THE
MINNESOTA
ROAD GUIDE
TO
MYSTERIOUS
CREATURES

THE
MINNESOTA
ROAD GUIDE
TO

MYSTERIOUS

CREATURES
By Chad Lewis

Samiha + Debrah

Happy haunted adventures to you

C

ISBN: 987-0-9824314-3-6

Proudly printed in the United States by Documation

On The Road Publications
3204 Venus Ave
Eau Claire, WI 54703
www.ontheroadpublications.com
chadlewis44@hotmail.com

Cover Design: Kevin Lee Nelson
Illustrations - Kevin Lee Nelson

DEDICATION

This guide is dedicated to my fellow legend trippers Noah Voss and Kevin Nelson who put the fictional Winchester brothers to shame!

TABLE OF CONTENTS

PREFACE

Report Your Experiences – his guide is set up for you to have an adventure. I recommend that all legend trippers bring along at least a camera and journal to document your findings.

Private Property – Unfortunately a couple of the locations listed in this book are on private property. Please respect the privacy of the owners and only view these places from the road. If you do venture onto private property please make sure that you have prior permission, otherwise you may end up with a hefty trespassing ticket to go along with your creature sighting.

Safety – Many of these cases come with a side dish of danger. Not only do you have to watch out for the appearance of these mysterious creatures, you also have to keep a keen eye out for other known dangerous animals. Keep in mind that many of these locations are out in the middle of nowhere, so always try to have someone with you in case of injuries and emergencies. At the very least make sure that you tell someone where you are going so if you don't return, we will at least know where to retrieve your mauled remains.

Accuracy - I have made every effort to ensure this guide is up current and accurate yet some errors will inevitably surface. If you find better directions, take better photos, or manage to capture one of these beasts please contact me so I can make the changes for future editions of this book.

Roadside Attractions - This guide is just the tip of the iceberg of your adventure. Getting to these locations is half the fun, and Minnesota is filled with so many oddities that you should never run out of places to explore. Allot some time to hit all of the odd roadside attractions that you will bump into along your adventure.

Outside the Norm – Veteran legend trippers know that the best adventures come by getting out of your daily routine. Travel the back roads, spend the night at the dodgy roadside motel, and grab a meal at the old mom and pop diner. Trust me the chain businesses will not miss you.

Acknowledgements

First and foremost I have to thank all of the people of Minnesota (both living and dead) who have kept these legends alive for all of us to enjoy.

This guide would not have been as complete without the aid and assistance of the dozens of librarians, researchers, and historians, who kindly lent their expertise and provided me with a wealth of information.

Once again I owe a huge debt of gratitude to Sarah Szymanski for helping to make this guide a wonderful resource for adventure.

A hearty thank goes out to Kevin Nelson for the wonderful illustrations that really cause the creatures to leap from the page.

All legend trippers need a base camp and in the Midwest you can find no better place than the Headhunter's Hideaway where no subject or case discussed is ever weirder than the people discussing it.

Since this book is all about adventure I have to give a huge thank you to the world's greatest legend trippers, Noah Voss, Kevin Nelson, Todd Roll, and Jesse Donahue who were on several of these amazing expeditions with me.

Finally, I want to thank my wife, Nisa Giaquinto, and our son Leo for being the best two creatures in the world to share a life with.

Introduction

In 2004, while living in Wisconsin I began traveling Minnesota while gathering research for the book, *The Minnesota Road Guide to Haunted Locations*. During my travels I had discovered so many haunted stories that I dubbed Minnesota "The Land of 10,000 Ghosts." Along the way I also collected various stories of mysterious creatures that were often intertwined with the haunted legends, yet remained on the outskirts of other well-known legends. With tales of Paul Bunyan and Babe his big blue ox, the Minnesota Iceman, and rabid Vikings fans, Minnesotans are no strangers to weird creatures. But there is something about the creatures in this guide that tend to place them on the fringe of belief. Science tells us they shouldn't exist, skeptics claim that can't exist, and yet every year hundreds of people came face to face with these "non-existent" creatures.

In my quest to discover these bizarre monsters I have traveled the entire state from top to bottom, I dug up the old records, interviewed witnesses, and prowled in places that shouldn't be prowled in. Along the way I found myself jumping into a freezing Lake Superior in search of the serpent, being nearly lulled to sleep by the little people of Pipestone, and covered in ticks as I made my way to an alleged Bigfoot nest, all in the pursuit of putting together a guide that would provide others the same opportunity to encounter the weird. Although definitive evidence may have eluded me, adventure certainly didn't, and that is what I believe is at the heart of this guide. When you travel to these locations hopefully you will have a paranormal experience, maybe you will maybe you won't, but I can assure you that you will have an adventure. Many of these locations are far off the beaten path which allows for some good old fashioned exploration. Take the back roads and you are guaranteed to meet some odd and interesting characters. Be sure to allot some extra time to stumble across Minnesota's wonderful assortment of unique roadside attractions where you could find yourself anywhere from the Birthplace of America in Alexandria to the Stained Glass Capitol of the World in Winona. Everywhere you wander you will be met with weirdness and hopefully along the way you might just discover that you are a little stranger than you gave yourself credit for.

Keep an eye out,

Chad Lewis

Pepie – The Serpent of Lake Pepin

Where To Encounter It:

Lake Pepin – Lake City, MN
www.pepie.net

Directions:

Lake Pepin runs along Minnesota's eastern border with Wisconsin. There are several great viewing areas and public lake access all the way down Highway 61 from Wacouta to Reeds Landing. However, the main destination for legend trippers is the official Pepie lookout town of Lake City.

Creature Lore:

Something unknown is lurking in Lake Pepin, and for over 140 years this mysterious creature has inhabited the largest lake on the Mississippi River. Just what this bizarre monster is remains unknown, as accounts seem to vary from witness to witness. The Native Americans believed that it was a dangerous killer, the old pioneers believed it was an undiscovered species, and modern vacationers see it as a tourist draw. Each year the long list of eyewitnesses continues to grow, while the answer to what this puzzling creature really is remains as far away as it ever has.

History of Lore:

Tales of the expansive lake hosting some unknown water beastie date back to the Native Americans who first settled near the area. Legend tells of the Natives holding a healthy respect for the many mysteries of the lake. Their respect eventually turned to avoidance after numerous canoes were attacked and punctured by some large water beast. The beautiful waters of Lake Pepin quickly gained the reputation of a place that housed something dark and deadly.

Although oral tales of the creatures date back much further, the first recorded sighting of the creature took place on April 24, 1871. According to the April 26 edition of the *Wabasha County Sentinel*, local residents Giles Hyde and C. Page Bonney reported seeing a large unidentified marine monster in the lake. The sensational sighting reported that the creature was between the size of an elephant and a rhinoceros, and it moved with great rapidity. The newspaper also stated that on several prior occasions the creature had also been spotted, but no further details were given. The possibilities of the true origin of the creature were endless; the paper even speculated that "the water in the lake is known to be very deep, whales might live in – but this is not likely to be a whale." Other newspapers picked up and expanded on the case, as the *Titusville Herald* out of Pennsylvania stated that Lake Pepin was "infested with a marine monster." While no definitive explanation of the creature was purposed, two aspects of the monster were widely agreed upon—it was big, and it was fast.

In 1875, the creature made several other spectacular appearances. The *Pierce County Herald* told of a couple of strange sightings that took place in July. The details of the first sighting are lacking, as unfortunately the paper only states that a monster of some kind was spotted opposite Lake City, Minnesota. The second account is a bit more detailed and tells of Mr. Hewitt and two boys who were out sailing from Lake City to Wacouta in a skiff, when about halfway to their destination, a "dark, strange-looking object rose out of the lake about six feet high at the stern of the boat." The beast remained out of the water long enough for the trio to get a detailed look at it before it disappeared into the depths of the lake. Again, the paper failed to list specific details such as its color, type of body, or other identifying marks. And while most of the town was buzzing with the monster news, not all were believers in Pepie. Several skeptical residents believed that the mysterious sighting was nothing more than a regular lake occupant of natural origin, similar to the four-foot-long, five-and-a-half-pound eel that had been captured in the lake just prior to the sighting.

Throughout the early 1900s, the sea serpent legend calmed down a bit and, like most legends, it was nearly forgotten. It wasn't until more recent sightings started occurring that the rich history of the lake brought the creature back into the limelight.

Investigation Log:

Having been on several expeditions in search of the Loch Ness Monster, I was immediately struck by the uncanny similarities that Lake Pepin shares with the infamous Scotland Loch. Both bodies of water are approximately 23 miles long, both are over a mile wide, and both are surrounded by beautiful bluffs. Although Lake Pepin is not quite as deep as Loch Ness, there is still plenty of room for aquatic mysteries to live. And while many experts believe that Loch Ness does not have a sufficient food source to sustain a population of large sea serpents, Lake Pepin is widely recognized for its plentiful fishing and would have no problem providing for a family of creatures.

Adding even more credibility to the sea serpent legend is the fact that throughout history Lake Pepin's large body of water has been filled with many other large aquatic animals. On August 10, 1891, the *Eau Claire Weekly Leader* ran the headline, "A Big Fish." The story told of a shovel-nosed sturgeon that had been caught in Lake Pepin. The sturgeon's 16 pound head was described as the largest head ever seen in the area. The fish itself weighed well over 85 pounds. Certainly a fish of this size could have caused quite a disturbance on the lake, leading many to believe that the sturgeon was solely responsible for many of the sea serpent sightings.

Photo of unknown object in the lake

The February 2, 1918 edition of the *La Crosse Tribune and Leader Press* featured a story of a mammoth sheephead fish being netted out of Lake Pepin. While a normal sized sheephead in the lake averaged one and a quarter pounds, this whopper weighed over 24 pounds. Even more remarkable than the weight was the sheer size of the fish, which measured over three feet long and had a girth of over one foot. If seen at the right distance, this giant sheephead certainly could have seemed like a large serpent.

In 2011, a gentleman contacted me looking to report a strange sighting that he had at Lake Pepin back in the 1970s while fishing with his two young children. Without a boat, the trio was forced to fish off of a rock jetty along the Wisconsin side of the lake. They were about half-way out on the jetty when "something lunged up breaking the surface of the water." Gray in color, the fisherman estimated it to be one foot in diameter while about three feet of its body showed above the water. At first the man believed it was a Muskie, however its mouth was "open in such a way as to resemble an open pipe." The reason for its surfacing became clear as a bird flying three feet over the water was snatched out of mid-air by the mysterious creature.

Something mysterious in the lake

The official Pepie website showcases several of the more interesting sightings that have been complied over the years. One such sighting took place on July 9, 2008. At approximately 10am, a motorist was traveling along on Highway 61 and noticed a very large creature moving parallel to the Lake City Beach. The witness pulled over to snap a photo of the creature, which was estimated to be somewhere between 30 and 40 feet long. After snapping the photo, the witness watched the creature slowly disappear back into the water.

On one of my expeditions to Lake Pepin, I spoke with a woman who vividly remembered her bizarre sighting of Pepie. On August 21, 2010, the woman and her husband were traveling along Highway 61 when something odd caught her attention. From the passenger window, she gazed out at Lake Pepin and noticed something moving in the water that resembled the long neck and head of a serpent. Not quite believing what she was seeing, the woman jokingly told her husband that she had just seen something that looked like Pepie. Her husband briefly turned his attention from the road to the lake and spotted the same creature. The couple estimated that—whatever the creature was—it had a neck and head that was sticking a good two feet out of the water. It also appeared that the head was attached to a larger body that was mostly submerged under the water. The sighting only lasted a few seconds, and the heavy traffic on the highway forced the couple to keep moving. It all happened so fast that they were not truly sure if they could believe their own eyes. The couple discussed the possibility that what they had seen was a dead log or other floating debris, and like so many others who have witnessed something strange in Lake Pepin, the couple chalked their sighting up as an unsolved mystery. It is safe to say that the various fish listed above undoubtedly accounted for some of the sightings throughout the years. Yet, it is equally safe to say to state that based on the sheer size and scope of the beast reported by eyewitnesses that something other than a few large fish has been living in the depths of Lake Pepin.

In 2011, I traveled to Lake Pepin along with fellow legend trippers Todd Roll, Noah Voss, Kevin Nelson, and Jesse Donahue. We charted a boat and our first step was to hit some of the locations where Pepie had been previously sighted. Our detailed fishing map also provided us with a few of the deeper spots around the lake where we decided to focus on these areas where the creature would have more room to maneuver or hide. We traveled up and down the lake, casted off some baited fishing lines, tried a conjuring spell, jumped in the water and searched, and generally kept an eye out for anything out of the ordinary. After many hours of encountering rolling waves, half submerged logs, and bathing birds, we ended up empty handed when it came to evidence of Pepie's existence. After all our research, planning, and searching we left Lake City hoping that if a monster does indeed dwell within Lake Pepin that it survives until our next expedition.

Postcard of the elusive Pepie.

Much to their credit, the town of Lake City has embraced the legend of Pepie. In fact, the downtown store of Treats & Treasures is an Official Pepie Watch Station and contains a lot of Pepie merchandise. I spoke with the shop's owner, who informed me that over the years many people have ventured into her store with their personal Pepie sightings. Local business owner Larry Nielson runs the Pepie website and is a wealth of knowledge on the history and sighting of the creature. Nielson and the town are so convinced that Pepie is real that they are offering a $50,000 reward to anyone who can capture proof of its existence. Good Luck!

Lake Superior Sea Serpent

Where To Encounter It:

Lake Superior

Directions:

The best opportunity to visit Lake Superior is along Minnesota's North Shore. From Duluth you can travel north on Highway 61 all the way to Canada with plenty of access points along the way.

Creature Lore:

The height of sea serpent reports came from the time period of the 1800s and early 1900s. During this period our lakes and oceans remained mostly unexplored and the bodies of water possessed unlimited amounts of danger, romance, and deadly creatures that dwarfed anything ever seen before. The sheer uniqueness of these creatures was limitless with tourists, fisherman, boat captains, and nearly everyone else who was in a frenzy over what lurked beneath the waters. Somewhere around the 1930s reports of sea serpents started to dwindle. Whether people stopped seeing them or the media stopped reporting them, serpent sightings all but vanished from the general public's awareness, leaving a giant mystery in their place. Where did all of these creatures go? Did they move deeper to avoid the approach of man, or had they become extinct? For decades reports of serpents remained a rare phenomenon. Yet recently, for some inexplicable reason sea serpent sightings are again on the rise, leading many legend trippers to grab their camera and head off to Lake Superior in search of the next great serpent sighting.

History of Lore:

The history of majestic Lake Superior is full of tales of something large and deadly inhabiting the seemingly unending body of water. Long before white pioneers settled the area Native Americans had already developed a healthy respect for the vicious creatures that dwelled in the lake. Oral tales from the natives told of unimaginably huge beasts that could swallow a man, or ship, with ease. If for any reason members of a tribe turned up missing, the disappearance was blamed on the serpents of the water. When the white pioneers finally moved into the area the exclusively oral tales shifted to that of the widely circulated newspaper, which in turn spread the tales of the serpents much further than ever before.

The expansive Lake Superior

On August 3, 1895, the *Ironwood News Record* wrote of the sensational sighting of the *S.S. Curry* during its trip down from Ashland, WI. The ship, under the direction of the "veracious" Captain George Robarge, was passing by White Fish Point at sunset when Robarge eyed a huge retile that "thrust his long neck above the water's surface" a mere 400 yards from the ship. For a full five minutes the beast kept pace with the boat which allotted the ship's crew enough time to grab their "glasses" and obtain a better look. With binoculars in hand, the crew could make out an extraordinarily large creature whose neck "was some 15 feet in length" with jaws that parted a good foot or more. The article stated that the men watched with trepidation as "every now and then its body partially rose above the waves and revealed a strange undulating motion" before disappearing into the dark of the water.

In 1897, the *Detroit News-Tribune* reported on a terrifying attack from a creature believed to be a giant squid. It happened as a ship was nearing the shallow waters around Duluth and struck what was thought to be a rock. One of the crewmen went to assess the damage of the collision when he tripped over a rope and landed in 10 feet of water. Immediately he was seized by the tentacles of a 70-foot green beast with "great scales and a forked tail." As his boat was being pushed out to sea the man appeared doomed to meet his fate as the creature's powerful grip tightened around his waist, sucking away his remaining air. As the man trashed about he could make out the beast's two giant eyes as he fought to gain footing on the lake bottom. After a mighty struggle the brave sailor somehow broke free and made his way to shore, happy to have survived his encounter with the unknown beast.

Investigation Log:

The North Shore of Minnesota is an extremely popular destination for tourists looking to relax near Lake Superior. As one of the state's most visited areas, a lot of eyes are cast onto the lake. It may come as no surprise that with so many people admiring the beauty of the water, sightings of the unexplained are bound to pop up.

Regardless of their belief in the paranormal the majority of people who visit Lake Superior leave the area with the belief that it is a magical and mystical place. Some believe this is caused by the calm and soothing sounds of the waves crashing against the shore while others experience a deeper more spiritual connection to the lake. As the largest of the Great Lakes, Superior offers plenty of space for weirdness to happen and the overwhelming majority of cases from the lake are not that of sea serpents, but that of phantom ships. It only seems logical when you consider that thousands of ships and crewmembers have met their end at the hands of the treacherous lake. Tales of tragic mishaps and disappearances are all too numerous on the unforgiving lake that has sent many of person to their watery graves where they are doomed to spend eternity. The problem lies in the fact that these victims, along with their ships, are not resting peacefully. In fact, each year dozens of unsuspecting vacationers report seeing the ghostly images of old 1800s looking ships sailing across the lake. And even though nothing beats the picture of these ghostly vessels moving silently though a fog- filled moonlit night, sightings of these phantom ships have been reported in both day and night, with or without fog.

During the late 1800s ships dreaded encounters with serpents

Outside of all the phantom ship sightings, sea serpents do occasionally get spotted as well. In their book *The Mysterious North Shore* authors William Mayo and Kate Barthel tell of a man who was visiting the area when he saw something he just couldn't explain. The man was checking out a spot near Stuart River where he had discovered a good view overlooking the river and lake. Standing on a small cliff the rose up over the lake the man noticed something in the lake that did not quite fit, explaining that he had seen something akin to a "really big fish or something" in the lake. Pressed for details the man reported that it "looked like a rock at first – or a turtle's back." A bit confused by what he had experienced the man continued with his story claiming that the creature "would submerge, and you could just make it out under the surface then it would move around and come back up." Trying to estimate the size of the mysterious creature the man spread out his arms as wide as they would go indicating that whatever he saw, it was pretty big. Sticking with the common response of many witnesses, the man quickly tried to explain away his sighting telling himself that it had to be a big fish or turtle, because what else could it be?

Every so often I will receive a sea serpent report from Lake Superior. Usually these reports are from those who only catch a quick glimpse of something that seems out of place in the lake. Mostly these sightings lack any real details due to their short exposure and end up in my unexplained pile because due to the insufficient details it is difficult to place them in a category. It is not the fault of the eyewitnesses it is just that these things happen so quickly that a perfect picture cannot be etched into our memory. I myself have spent a lot of time out on Lake Superior in search of sea serpents and many things have caught my eye as I scanned the water, unfortunately none of them turned out to be a sea serpent.

Plenty of room for an undiscovered monster to dwell?

On your next trip to Lake Superior you may want to avert your eyes from the water and focus on the sky because a lot of UFOs have also been seen flying over the lake. Tales of mysterious buzzing lights, hovering objects, and unknown aircraft are plentiful along Lake Superior. With reports of phantom boats, giant monster lurking in the water, and UFOs flying overhead, you may just find yourself joining the long list of those who believe there is something truly magical about Lake Superior.

The Phantom Cats of
Miller's Anoka Cafe

Where To Encounter It:

Miller's Anoka Cafe

1918 1st Ave.

Anoka, MN

(763) 712-0824

Directions:

The cafe is located in the heart of downtown Anoka, just off of East
Main Street.

Creature Lore:

Cats have always had a close association with the paranormal, dating back to the Egyptians who saw them as sacred creatures that were to be revered as such. Here in the United States, cats— especially black ones—were thought to be in cahoots with the Devil, aligning themselves with the black magic of witches. Early folklorists recorded the expressed beliefs among many cultures that supernatural creatures like vampires and witches possessed the ability to shape-shift and take on the form of a cat. Today our views of cats being sinister creatures of the night have softened a bit, as cats have become a favorite domesticated family pet. Many people consider their cats part of their family and are heartbroken when their pet passes on. With such a close connection to our felines, it comes as no surprise that these animals have had a long history of being ghostly apparitions.

History of Lore:

Like any good Hollywood movie, there is much speculation that the land on which Miller's Anoka Cafe occupies was at one time used as a Native American burial ground, a claim that I have not been able to confirm nor debunk.

The Anoka Café building was constructed back in 1888 and stories of it being a place in which paranormal activity occurred soon followed. Over the years, the building has seen a long list of various businesses come and go, and with each new occupant came fresh stories of odd events that took place. Back in 2005, I spoke with a long time resident of Anoka who told me that when she was a young child her family used to get their milk from the creamery that operated out of the building's basement. The young girl dreaded the errand, for she was the one expected to walk down to the basement to pick up the milk in the place which had such a well-known reputation for being haunted.

Many restaurants have also passed through the building, including the River Front, D Eatery, RNB's, Cully's, and others, but it wasn't until the restaurant was Cal's Corner Café that all of the supernatural stories began to leak out.

Investigation Log:

It seems truly fitting that the town of Anoka, which prides itself on being the Halloween Capital of the World, would be filled with reports of phantom cats—the animal most closely tied to Halloween—roaming its downtown. But as you will soon discover, there is so much paranormal activity happening at Miller's Anoka Café that the town may just live up to is proclaimed Halloween Capital moniker.

Site where the phantom cats have been seen and heard

In 2005, while working on the book *The Minnesota Road Guide to Haunted Locations*, I visited the restaurant, which at the time was called Cal's Corner Café. During my investigation, I spoke with the owner, Cal, and several of his employees. In talking with the employees, I was amazed at the sheer amount of different phenomena that was talking place at the restaurant. Outside of the phantom cats, which I will get to in a bit, the place was flooded with strange happenings. At the time of my investigation, Cal had only owned the place for a couple of years, yet he was well aware of many bizarre stories dating back to previous owners. One of his main concerns was that his place was going to be robbed during the middle of the night. The reason for this seemingly illogical fear came from the fact that at the end of every day he shut off all the lights, locked up, and exited through the front door. Yet, somehow, when he returned first thing in the morning, the front door was often found unlocked, and all of the lights had been turned back on.

As we talked, Cal began to open up and share some even stranger stories that he had personally encountered. One evening while alone in the restaurant, he was downstairs making an inventory of his supplies when the silence was broken by what sounded like young girls whispering secrets to one another. He could hear the sounds but was unable to decipher what the voices were saying. Making things even more bizarre was the fact that Cal was certain that the whispering was coming from behind a heavy locked storage door. As he slowly crept toward the noise, he cautiously put his ear up against the door to listen and again heard the whispering. Seeing the seriousness in his eyes as he recounted the story, I couldn't wait any longer and quickly asked if he found anyone when he opened the door. Cal looked at me as though I was crazy and said, "I didn't open up that door. I took off upstairs as fast as I could." It is fitting to note that out of all the events customers have reported experiencing, hearing odd noises coming from the basement was at the top of the list. After having experienced so many odd things at the restaurant, one female employee decided to hold a group séance in the basement, with the hope that it might shine some light onto the cause of all the mysterious happenings. While nothing much surfaced in the basement, the group swore that they could hear someone walking around upstairs. As they rushed up to investigate they found the room completely empty, but strangely all of the Christmas tree lights had mysteriously turned on by themselves.

By then the staff was paying more attention to their work surroundings, which only seemed to increase the frequency of the paranormal activity. One employee was busy cooking when he experienced the strange sensation that someone, or something, was standing right next to him. A bit startled, the man spun around— only to discover that no one was there. Moments later, the cook's apron came untied as though the strings were pulled by some unseen force.

It was common that before closing down for the day the staff would prepare the restaurant for the following morning's breakfast. This usually included setting out the silverware, filling up the condiments, and washing down the tables. On several occasions, all of their preparation was thwarted when the morning staff came in to discover that all of the silverware, along with the salt and pepper shakers, had been neatly stacked onto one table. The mischievous culprit responsible for re-arranging things was never discovered.

Amongst all the various odd happenings that have taken place at the building, by far the weirdest is that of the phantom cat(s) that have been seen and heard by both staff and unsuspecting customers. While working away inside the restaurant, staff members would often hear the sound of a cat's meowing coming from the basement. Thinking that maybe a stray cat had somehow found its way into the building, the workers would venture downstairs to check it out and would be surprised to find the basement empty and quiet. Most of the customers that frequent the cafe are gleefully unaware of the supernatural happenings that have taken place. Many just stop in to enjoy a good meal and conversation among friends. Not only have these customers commented about hearing a cat meowing throughout the building, many have actually caught a glimpse of it. Staff members told me that on several different occasions while up at the cash register paying for their meals, customers commented about how much they liked the restaurant's cat and inquired about its name. With hushed voices, the workers had to tell them that there were no cats inside the restaurant…at least not any that were living!

The Phantom Pig of the Minnesota State Fair

Where To Encounter It:

Minnesota State Fair
1265 North Snelling Ave. N.
St. Paul, MN

Directions:

From Interstate 94, turn north on Snelling Avenue; follow Snelling
and the park grounds will be on the left.

Creature Lore:

Believe it or not, in the field of paranormal research, hearing stories about a phantom pig is not that out of the ordinary. Throughout my years of research, I have investigated a myriad of phantom creatures from mundane phantom cats and dogs to more exotic phantom animals like elephants and kangaroos. When I first heard tales of a disappearing spectral pig inhabiting the Minnesota State Fair, I scoured through my case files trying to locate any similar reports. Reports of phantom pigs are fairly scarce, but a few years back in Door County, Wisconsin, I investigated a local legend that told of a backfired curse that created pigs with human faces…yet these pigs weren't phantoms, they were said to have been flesh and blood. My only other encounter with pigs came during an expedition in Florida where, while searching the Everglades for a Bigfoot type creature called the Skunk Ape, I found myself face to snout with several wild feral pigs. Although these pigs were dangerous, they were by no means supernatural…making this state fair case my first endeavor into actual ghost pigs.

History of Lore:

At a time when most families in America were involved in farming, raising pigs was an essential part of everyday life. As the number of swine being raised continued to rise, so did the odd stories associated with them. Tales of pigs being born with physical deformities made for interesting newspaper stories and often these abnormal pigs would bring a nice little profit from one of the numerous dime museums that displayed such freaks of nature. In 1872, the *Janesville Gazette* wrote about a "monstrosity" of a pig being born in Platteville, Wisconsin, where in addition to its "eight legs, four ears, one eye-socket with three eye balls," it also had an elephant's trunk projecting out from its forehead.

In 1974, police in Victoria, Texas were called out in search of a "phantom porker" after residents complained of a wild pig terrorizing the place, putting the entire neighborhood on edge. It is unclear just what the residents were seeing, as the *Victoria Advocate* wrote, "Neighbors in the area also reported seeing the phantom pig," yet "Officer Theus was not able to locate the animal." No follow-up article was found and it is not known if the phantom porker was ever apprehended or is still out there causing trouble in Texas.

More recently, I received a report from a gentleman in Texas who had taken his family out for a drive through the back roads of the countryside. While cruising along, the family spotted what he called "the strangest creature we have ever seen." The man described the creature as being the size of a full-grown pig with the body of a rat (tail included). As the family got a closer look, they noticed that the creature had white prickled skin and its eyes were shut. The family was able to gather a good look at the creature before they quickly exited the area.

Just how long the phantom pigs have been roaming the state fair is difficult to ascertain. The fair itself has been operating since 1855, only missing five years in its entire 150 year history. In 1885, the fair was moved from its various roving sites to its current location. I first started receiving reports of the phantom pig back around 2000. It is entirely possible that these phantom pigs have been plaguing the fair since its inception.

Investigation Log:

It is a giant understatement to say that weirdness is afoot at the Minnesota State Fair. Aside from the deep fried candy bars and the wacky funhouse, the fair is also home to frequent encounters with wandering ghosts, phantom creatures, and reincarnated birds. Each year the fair attracts over one-and-a-half-million visitors, the majority of which leave the fair with nothing more than an upset stomach and an oversized stuffed animal prize. Yet, underneath this seemingly wholesome adventure are those visitors who exit the fairgrounds after having come face to face with the paranormal. Among the whirling rides, games of chance, and dazzling attractions are three separate phenomena that you should keep an eye out for.

One of the empty pens where the phantom pig appears.

The first oddity of the fair is the wandering ghost of a man whose identity and purpose remain unknown. Over the years, this spirit has been spotted throughout the entire fairgrounds, but the majority of sightings take place near the grandstand. This is where the big-name entertainment performs, leading many to speculate that perhaps the spirit is that of a former security guard or fair employee. But then again, the spirit may just enjoy being around all the action. Both the *St. Paul Pioneer Press* and the *Minneapolis Star Tribune* have featured stories from surprised visitors who have crossed paths with the phantom fairgoer as he made his way around the grounds…only to disappear right before their eyes.

The second oddity of the fair involves Wayne Murray, a long-time employee of the fair who took his job at the Ye Old Mill very seriously. The Ye Old Mill was one of the oldest rides at the fair and provided customers with the opportunity to leisurely float through a historic-looking mill in small rickety boats. The ride was a throwback to the early days of Minnesota, and every year Murray looked forward to ensuring that everyone had a great time on the attraction. Eventually Murray passed away, but some believe that he hasn't let death impede on his yearly work ritual. On the first day of the fair following Murray's death, employees noticed a strange black bird that descended from the sky and landed on the Ye Old Mill sign. The odd bird stayed at the ride for sometime before departing back to the sky. The next year on the first day of the fair the mysterious bird once again showed up at the ride, stayed a bit, and then disappeared just as it did the year before. As the years passed, and the bird kept showing up, the legend began to grow that the bird was the reincarnated spirit of Murray returning to his beloved ride in order to check up on things. I spoke with several employees of the ride who all had heard the story, although none of them had witnessed the bird for themselves. It is also unclear whether the bird is a normal flesh and blood creature or some type of spirit bird.

A real pig housed at the fair

The final paranormal piece of the fair comes at one of the main attractions. The livestock barns are where thousands of animals are brought in to be shown, judged, and admired. On any given day, you can easily run across scores of cows, ducks, geese, goats, horses, llamas, pigs, rabbits, and turkeys as they overflow the barns. The fair organizes plenty of activities around these animals, including animal care lectures, horse riding events, and even a petting zoo where you can get an up-close look at the creatures. Among all of these blue ribbon winners, one creature seems to completely stand out from the rest. Witnesses who visit the swine barn often get more than they bargained for when they notice a phantom pig inside one of the pens. At first glance the pig appears like every other normal pig. Upon further inspections, they notice that this pig is nearly transparent and they almost see right through it. The sightings of this creature are fleeting, because it tends to disappear right into thin air. Over the years, a legend began to surface that no matter how many times you try, or how many cameras you use, you would not be able to snap a photo of the phantom pig. I spent a lot of time at the fair speaking with those at the swine barn and was unable to locate anyone with a personal experience of the pig, even though many of them were familiar with the legend.

With such a variety of phenomena talking place here, the fair makes for a wonderful paranormal legend trip. However, you do have to plan a bit to time this one right, because the Minnesota State Fair is a rare case when you only have a limited window of time to experience the legends. The fair itself only operates for 12 days beginning in late August and ending every year on Labor Day.

Spectral Dog of Oneota Cemetery

Where To Encounter It:

Oneota Cemetery
6403 Highland Street
Duluth, MN 55807-1136
(218) 624-1932

Directions:

From I-35S, take exit 252 (Central Ave.). Turn right (north) on Central and follow it for approximately one mile. Turn left on Highland Street, follow it for one-half mile, and you will reach the cemetery.

Creature Lore:

Phantom animals are being reported so frequently that they are starting to rival their deceased human counterparts. Just in this guide alone you will be able to find your way to several spectral dogs, cats, and even pigs. Many cultures around the world believe that the spirit of animals, like humans, continue to exist in the afterlife. Unlike numerous other tales of phantom animals, this case is slightly more intriguing due to the addition of a ghostly man that not only accompanies the dog, he seems to exert some kind of supernatural control over it. The problem with investigating ghostly animals lies in the difficulty of identifying anything about them. All the usual avenues of researching property deeds, death records, marriage licenses, etc. do absolutely no good when trying to pin down the identity of a wondering phantom animal. Perhaps the more important question does not hinge on the identity of the dog, but rather why it continues to roam the cemetery from the afterlife.

History of Lore:

The cemetery itself dates back to 1885 and is the final resting place for many Minnesota pioneer families and soldiers. It is entirely possible that the legend of the phantom dog predates the cemetery. Most likely the 100 acres of land that now comprise the cemetery grounds overlooking the St. Louis River basin were at one time used as farmland or homesteading. The precise origin of the legend is unknown, as it only widely surfaced a few years ago. Just how far back into time the legend goes is still undetermined.

Investigation Log:

The legend of the Oneota Cemetery tells of the graveyard being inhabited by a disappearing phantom dog and its ghostly master.

The picturesque cemetery houses many old gravesites dating back to the late 1800s, making it a hotspot for local history buffs. At night the scenic, historic graveyard which overlooks the St. Louis River Basin takes on a more devious tone. For years the legend was rarely told and only known to a handful of local residents until it was featured in the book *The Mysterious North Shore* by William Mayo and Kate Barthel. In their book, the authors uncovered two different accounts of the wandering dog and the equally mysterious "man" who is spotted alongside it.

Embankment where the mysterious man and his dog disappear

The first account took place in 1992 when a group of teenagers decided to take a legend trip out to the old cemetery in hopes of experiencing something out of the ordinary. Upon arrival, the group spread out and quickly became engrossed in reading the names and dates on many of the old grave markers under the glowing light of the moon. Suddenly, the sounds of an approaching visitor broke the quiet night air. Knowing that the cemetery officially closed at dusk, the group promptly found hiding spots—afraid that the approaching person was an angry caretaker looking to kick them out, or even worse, a police officer looking to fine them for trespassing. As he cautiously peeked out from behind a large gravestone, one of the boys could see the strange, dark figure of a tall man being led by a muscular dog as it trotted through the cemetery. As the unknown duo passed directly in front of him, the hiding boy swore that he could hear the faint jingling of the dog's tags as it passed by. Relived that they had escaped any possible punishment, the group watched as the man and his dog continued about their business down the road. But instead of following the road back to the rest of the cemetery, the strange visitors simply kept walking into a patch of heavy brush that lined the steep drop off. After only a couple of audible steps through the brush, both the man and his dog simply vanished from sight.

The phantom hound of the cemetery

Mayo and Barthel also collected another puzzling account, again from 1992, in which they tell of a group of high school friends that had gathered next to the cemetery to hang out and listen to music for the evening. The group assumed that the road, which ran alongside the cemetery, would provide them with plenty of privacy from the prying eyes of any adult supervision. Yet shortly after arriving, the group spotted the figure of a man walking his dog down the road. While wondering what kind of weirdo would be out walking their dog so late at night, the friends watched as the snarling dog broke away from the man and came barreling towards them with its teeth on full display. What happened next was hard for the group to believe because, without so much as a whisper, the mysterious man simply raised his arm up in a circular motion, an action that immediately sent the dog rushing back to its master. Upon the dog's return, the two of them vanished over the steep overlook (the exact same area where the other group lost sight of the spirits). Needless to say, the party was cut short—the frightened friends high-tailed it out of the cemetery as fast as they could.

With two very similar accounts transpiring at the cemetery, the identity of the disappearing dog and its master still remains a mystery. There are numerous possible explanations for the phenomenon. Perhaps it is the spirit of a former cemetery caretaker and his dog who continue to perform their nightly watch duties, even from the grave. Or maybe the man and dog pre-date the land being used as cemetery and are the spirits of a pioneer family that once farmed the land. It is possible that the man once lived somewhere nearby and had grown accustomed to walking his dog through the cemetery, a ritual that they still repeat after death. We also cannot rule out the chance that the witnesses were mistaken in their sightings and that the man and his dog were perfectly normal living beings that happened to be out for an evening walk. After visiting and investigating the cemetery for myself, I am less inclined to subscribe to the latter theory because of the extreme difficulty of navigating the sheer drop-off where the man and dog reportedly disappeared. It seems highly unlikely that anyone would choose to take this off-road route in the daytime, much less during the darkness of the evening.

Perfect spot for a ghost to walk his phantom dog

Another interesting aspect of this case deals with the lack of any apparent awareness or acknowledgement between the phantom man and any of the witnesses. On both occasions, the man seemed to be oblivious of the fact that other people were in the cemetery. Usually any type of limited interaction between the spirit and the witness would ensure that the case be classified as a residual haunting, meaning that the phenomenon is most likely a past event that is being replayed over and over—much like a recorded show with the character(s) engaging in the exact same behavior during each subsequent sighting. However, the dog did/does seem aware of outside factors, as on at least one occasion it raced its way toward the group of parked partiers–only to be called off by the seemingly supernatural wave of its master's beckoning hand. With the identity of both the dog and its master all but lost to history, this case may remain unexplained for many years to come.

Aliens Attack in Sauk Centre

Where To Encounter It:

Truckers Inn
1420 Main Street South
Sauk Centre, MN
(320) 352-5241

Guest House Inn
322 12th Street South
Sauk Centre, MN
(320) 351-7256
www.guesthouseintl.com/hotels/saukcentre

Directions:

Truckers Inn is located at the intersection of Interstate 94 and Highway 71 (Main Street).

Guest House Inn – From 94 take Highway 71 (Main Street) toward downtown Sauk Centre. Turn right on 12th St. S (County Road 186). The hotel will be on your left side.

Creature Lore:

The creatures in this case are extremely difficult to classify due to the fact that they seemed to change shape and form throughout the encounter. The witnesses stated that the bizarre alien creatures took the form of something that appeared like small prehistoric birds. To make matters even more bizarre, the mysterious creatures were only eight-inches tall with v-shaped heads and flew around with wings on their backs. Throughout this case, I classify the creatures as "aliens" based on the original description by the witnesses who were convinced these things were extraterrestrial beings. However, if it wasn't for the appearance of several flying ships, one could make a strong case that with the general description of the creatures...along with their supposed shape-shifting abilities... that perhaps they would be more accurately described as fairies, or gnome-like creatures. Regardless of what we actually call these creatures, the witnesses reported that they could turn invisible, shape-shift, move at extraordinary speeds, and break the laws of physics, all of which are common abilities attributed to legendary folklore creatures.

History of Lore:

Throughout history, folklore has been filled with odd tales of mysterious creatures appearing in countless different forms. Fairies routinely appeared in the form of small bird or butterfly-like creatures, aliens have been remembered by abductees as being owls, deer, and giant squirrels, angels often took the form of bright light, and gnomes and little people are thought to have the ability to appear in the form of beautiful women. All of these are elaborate ruse attempted to disguise themselves from the prying eyes of humans. Since the beginning of recorded history, cultures around the world have encountered creatures for which they have no evidence and no explanation of their existence. Similar to how we currently view the Greek gods, in today's world most of these creatures are routinely brushed off as being nothing more than folklore legends created to explain events that rudimentary science was unable to. Yet, others looked to these cases as proof that the world was once full of many undiscovered creatures, and they hold on to the hope that perhaps it still is.

Truck stop where the frightened drivers sought safety

Investigation Log:

You can imagine the sheer amount of bizarreness that truck drivers encounter while traveling the interstates and highways of America. The freedom of the open road, the ability to see the ins and outs of the country, and the boundless possibilities of adventure combine to paint an attractive picture of driving a big rig. In reality, truckers have to contend with congested traffic, never ending greasy spoons, relentless hours, and alien-type creatures tormenting them across several state lines. That last one is exactly what plagued Bob and

Jackie Bair in 1984 as they gassed up their freshly painted truck in Seattle and set off to Madison, Wisconsin to deliver a truckload of vegetable oil. Three days later, the frazzled couple rolled into Sauk Centre claiming that unknown alien-type beings had been tormenting them for hundreds of miles. Pulling into the Truckers Inn café, the couple's amazing story quickly spread through town, eventually reaching local reporter Roberta Olson, who interviewed the pair for an article for the *Sauk Centre Herald*. With trembling hands and shaky voices, Bob and Jackie told Roberta the following story.

Things were moving along nice and smooth all the way until the couple reached Montana. It was just before daybreak and a few miles ahead of the rig the couple spotted several lights moving in the sky. At first the couple paid little attention to the lights, deeming them to be nothing more than the lights of a normal airplane flying across the sky. As the lights continued to move, they began to morph into nine little ships accompanied by one larger ship that was moving up and down in a lurching manner. A bit shaken by the transformation of the lights, the couple was anxious to escape the sighting and continued on their route hoping to stay on track with their delivery. In the span of a few seconds the couple realized that they weren't alone. Somehow the ship had continued to track the couple as they rolled out of the area. Amazingly, the lights had transformed once again, this time appearing the shape of tiny "eight inch people with V-shaped heads." The creatures were flying so close to the rig that Bob was able to see that they had small wings on their backs. Bob and Jackie silently wondered about the aliens' agenda when the encounter began to take a hostile turn for the worse. As the creatures swarmed around the truck, they began shooting "fine needle-like shavings like silver metal through the glass of the windshield." Maneuvering in his seat for a better look

Bob was amazed to see that the aliens "were shaped like a pre-historic bird." Now fully alarmed, Bob punched the accelerator with the hopeful belief that speed could distance him from the bird-like attackers. Little did the couple know that the bizarre encounter with these unknown creatures was only just beginning.

The truck as it looked after the attack

After driving for several uneventful miles, the couple quickly became distraught as they noticed that the ships were once again hovering sinisterly above them. The sky began to darken as the couple noticed thousands of "little black things" coming out of the sky. Soon the "squiggly things" began to appear everywhere. Bob stated that at that point in time he "didn't think it would harm any of us," but just as a precaution he continued to hit the gas reaching speeds over 70 miles per hour. Regardless of his speed, the lights were able to easily keep pace with him. While racing down the highway, Bob noticed that other objects resembling "vitamin E capsules" began to form on their windshield, spreading so quickly that the entire inside frame of the truck was covered with them. Determined to solve this mystery, the couple pulled over and attempted to gather a better look at what was attacking them. Frustratingly, whenever Bob stopped, the creatures stopped and flocked together as though playing some sort of twisted game of hide and seek. Without fail, as soon as the rig took off again, the aliens followed.

Finally, after three days of non-stop harassment, the Bair family made it to the safety of Sauk Centre. Pulling in to the Truckers Inn, the couple caused a sensation as they hurriedly told their story to those inside. Soon a crowd of people began to gather outside, including Police Chief George Trierweiler and an officer from the State Patrol. Bob and Jackie frantically tried to point out the aliens, who Bob said were hiding in the nearby trees. Although neither of the officers was able to see the lurking aliens, Chief Trierweiler told the *Sauk Centre Herald* that both witnesses were "very scared people." The lack of corroborating witnesses led Bob to believe that perhaps the aliens were invisible and only made themselves known to him and his wife. Looking to calm down, Bob and Jackie were persuaded to go inside and grab a booth. Seeking comfort in coffee and cigarettes, the couple tried to will their shaking hands into drawing sketches of the creatures. Bob also cautioned against touching any of the metal shavings that were shot at them, stating "every time I touched them I got blisters on my fingers." Flipping over one of his wrists he showed Roberta a large blister that had appeared after coming in contact with the unknown metal. Not knowing the true nature of what was happening to him, Bob speculated, "We might be dying right now! We don't know what it is, we need to get to a doctor." The more the couple spoke about the incident, the more fearful they became. Bob finally stated, "I'm scared to leave," a fear that prompted them to call their boss, who suggested that the obviously shaken couple get a motel room for the night.

Praying that a good night's rest would erase this horrific nightmare, Bob and Jackie checked into the nearby Travel Host Motel (Now the Guest House Inn). Unfortunately, the couple's prayers went unanswered and the supernatural activity continued inside their room. The couple reported that unknown metal fillings suddenly appeared in the bedspreads and the same Vitamin E-like capsules were now forming in their shower. Strangely, the motel manager reported that by all accounts the couple seemed perfectly normal and showed no visible signs of being distraught, nor did the couple report anything usual to him. Finally reaching their breaking point, Bob and Jackie refused to continue any farther on their own. Noting their fear, the trucking company sent a relief driver to Sauk Centre, and a few days later witnesses reported seeing the rig take off with the new guy behind the wheel and Bob in the passenger seat. Jackie was seen following closely behind in a rental car.

Too terrified to drive the truckers spent the night at this hotel

In addition to all the other material in the case, perhaps the most intriguing evidence was the truck itself. When the truck left Seattle, it had recently been painted and looked like a brand new rig. By the time it had reached Sauk Centre, the thing was pockmarked with small holes and chips that had wreaked havoc on the paint job. Bob claimed that the paint damage had been caused by the constant bombardment of the aliens that attacked them with metal projectiles. The *Sauk Centre Herald* wrote that "people from the Seattle, Wash. UFO Center," (most likely the National UFO Reporting Center) were in the process of investigating the case. Apparently the investigators "checked the truck all over and gathered evidence," but what eventually became of any discovered evidence is still unknown.

Needless to say, this was one extremely odd case to investigate. With so many extraordinary events only witnessed by Bob and Jackie, it is nearly impossible to ascertain what really happened back in 1984. My attempt to locate the original police report ended in disappointment when I discovered that the Sauk Centre Police only had reports dating back to 1992. I wasn't too surprised by the lack of the old record because it is an all too common problem when trying to deal with older cases. The rest of the world has reports going back hundreds of years while here in the U.S you will be lucky to find any report before the computer era. Without the police report, I decided to try and track down Chief George Trierweiler for an interview. Talking with him, I found that George, now retired from the force, had a somewhat different perspective on the bizarre case. When Bob was in the truck stop parking lot trying to point out the aliens to the curious crowd, George told me that he was right alongside Bob the entire time and that "there were no aliens there." George remembers that Bob was "talking out of his mind," as he ranted and raved about the aliens that no one else could see. George told me that both he and the other law enforcement agent believed that the couple were obliviously "under the influence of some type of 'hallucinogenic'" and had simply "taken too many pills." George was adamant in his belief that no aliens were terrorizing Sauk Centre.

In order to attempt to get closer to the truth, I also interviewed Roberta Olson, the *Sauk Centre Herald* reporter who had been the first investigator on the case. Even after all these years, Roberta could still clearly recall the level of fear that Bob and Jackie had displayed. Roberta informed me that when Bob pointed to show where the aliens were hiding, she was able to make out some type of dark form in amongst the trees, but she didn't move any closer because she "had little children at home and didn't want to take any chances." Even after her detailed investigation, Roberta is still unsure as to what exactly the couple really saw. In a fitting end to our interview, Roberta told me that she certainly "believes that there are things in the world that we don't know about."

My next stop was the Truckers Inn gas station and restaurant. I wanted to see if anyone there had remembered the story. Much to my surprise, I spoke with a long-time manager of the place who had actually started working at the stop shortly after the bizarre alien incident. He remembered that the whole place was abuzz with speculation over what transpired. Eventually the commotion of the event died down and gradually began to fade from the memory of the truck stop patrons.

From the Truckers Inn, I headed across the interstate to the Guest House Inn (originally the Travel Rest Motel). I was greeted by the proprietor of the place, Evy Schilling, who had purchased the hotel back in 2010. Unfortunately, the actual room that Bob and Jackie stayed in has been lost to history. Even though the hotel has undergone major modern upgrades, the layout and structure of the building appears much like it did in 1984, giving you the unique opportunity to book a room and discover for yourself if any aliens are still terrorizing Sauk Centre.

The alien attack continued inside their motel room

Howard Lake Spaceman

Where To Encounter It:

County Road 6 between Winsted and Howard Lake

Directions:

From Howard Lake travel south along County Road 6 (7th Ave) toward Winsted and you will be in the area where the sighting took place.

Creature Lore:

Out of all the strange creatures featured in this guide none come with more potential ramifications to our society than extraterrestrials. Imagine the devastating effects that it would bring to our economy, religion, culture, and quite possibly every other facet of our lives if it was announced that indeed alien beings have been interacting with us for a long time. You only need to take a quick look at the craziness that infected so many over the Y2K fiasco to get a sense of the scale we are looking at. Luckily for us, no extraterrestrial beings have made their presence known (that we are aware of). On the contrary, what we have are a series of bizarre encounters with unknown beings that when taken separately seem ridiculous, yet when compiled into a giant file of unexplained encounters you start to get a sense that maybe a major enouncement is not really necessary.

History of Lore:

During the 1940s the Howard Lake area was a hotbed of UFO activity. In 2003, *Herald Journal* reporter Lynda Jensen sought to connect with any living witnesses to the 1940s flap. Upon calling the Herald in 2011, I was told that Lynda Jensen has passed away and that no one was certain if she had even received any eyewitness UFO reports, and if she did, the whereabouts of such reports were unknown. I am currently still scouring through the old 1940s Howard Lake newspaper hoping to find any related articles.

Showing evidence of a previous flap of UFO sightings was the August 4, 1949 *Howard Lake Herald* article headline "Another Saucer?" which reported that on August 2, at around 7 a.m. a small brightly shining object appeared east of Howard Lake. The mysterious object reflected the sun's bright rays giving it a nearly transparent look. Witnesses claimed that "it was moving so slowly that at times it seemed to be standing still." Whatever the object was it did not fit into the normal saucer shaped craft that were so frequently reported during this time period, but instead it had a rounded top that came to a sharp point at the bottom. It must have been a busy news day in Howard Lake because the article included no further information on the bizarre sighting.

A few years later in 1952, the Herald ran another UFO story, this one titled "Flying Saucers Appear Near Howard Lake." The article tells of the fascinating sighting of Mr. and Mrs. Ed Rausch, who while enjoying a wonderful evening at their home near Mud Lake spotted two large "discs of light" in the sky. The lights which were estimated to be between three and four feet in diameter were circling the lake. The objects looked as though they were involved in some sort of bizarre game of tag as they chased after each other while momentarily disappearing from sight only to pop back into view to resume their circling orbit. Another resident of the home, Mrs. Dale Koenig, stepped outside to see the odd aerial display and watched along as the lights continued to dance in the sky. The curious group continued to observe the lights for quite some time but was unable to say what finally became of them.

Investigation Log:

Up until 1967 all of the reported sightings throughout the Howard Lake area were nothing more than CE1s (Close Encounter of the First Kind) in which only bizarre lights or crafts were spotted in the sky. The UFO activity that had been appearing in the area for a couple decades was about to get much more bizarre.

It was 4:30 in the morning when Harold Lenz began his daily work drive to the nearby town of Winsted. While passing through

Howard Lake his engine suddenly started to sputter and stalled out on him bringing his pickup truck to a halt. Lenz popped the hood and got out to assess the problem. Walking to the front of the vehicle, he spotted a luminous object that began to approach him. As the seventy-foot long, thirty -foot wide object got close Lenz could hear a strange whirling noise coming from the ship as it set down on three legs. Suddenly a bizarre looking elevator device came down from the bottom of the ship and before he could even react Lenz noticed a man-type being descend from the bottom of the ship. The average sized human looking creature was dressed in a tight-fitting silverfish blue uniform. But the oddest part was that the being seemed to have some sort of fish-bowl type helmet covering his head. The man, or creature, seemed oblivious to Lenz and appeared to be preoccupied with something on the underside of the craft. After careful inspection of the craft, the being simply headed back to the UFO and took off out of sight.

Location of the odd spaceman encounter

The case came from the United States Air Forces' Project Blue Book files which universally looked upon cases of human-alien encounters as being hoaxes, hallucinations, or misidentifications of things that had a more rational explanation. Back then their thinking was that any case where the witness(es) purportedly saw aliens was so preposterous that it should be thrown out without any thorough investigation. Due to this policy little else about this case is known. I have not been able to track down Harold Lenz to get his take on the event. Either Lenz moved away from the area or passed away because none of the residents, newspaper reporters, or business owners that I spoke with seemed to recall his name. As far as I have been able to tell the sighting was not covered by any of the local papers or media. With no available witness, no additional details, and no physical evidence skeptics claim that the entire case was nothing more than a hoax, which seems to be in direct contrast to the decades of UFO sightings throughout the area. As frustrating as it is, this case still remains unexplained, and until someone else encounters this odd looking fish bowl wearing man, we may never know the truth.

Flying Saucers Appear Near Howard Lake

Thursday evening about 9 o'clock Mr. and Mrs. Ed. Rausch witnessed a weird spectacle while at their home in the east end of town. Two large discs of light which seemed to be about three or four feet in diameter, were circling around over Mud lake, which adjoins their property on the east. They circled over the lake and disappeared beyond the trees, then reappeared, one following the other, in the same orbit. Mrs. Dale Koenig, who lives in an apartment in the Rausch residence, also came outside and watched the lights. The apparitions, whatever they were, were in evidence for as long as the Rausches stayed out to watch them and what finally became of them they do not know.

Newspaper account detailing the area's history of UFO sightings

Long Prairie Aliens

Where To Encounter It:

Highway 27
Long Prairie, MN

Directions:

From Long Prairie head east on Highway 27 for 4 miles and you
will be where the sighting took place. Keep in mind the road has
changed several times, so the original curve is no longer there.

Creature Lore:

Reports of UFOs come in all different shapes (non-shapes), sizes, and colors. Everything from long, cigar-shaped objects to the traditional saucer-looking craft to balls of lights that seem to maneuver under the control of some unseen control...odd flying objects are routinely being reported. In fact, the only thing that varies as widely as UFO reports is that of the occupants often seen inside the UFOs. The UFO literature is overflowing with strange accounts that involve even stranger creatures. For me, the truly fascinating cases include the sighting of some creature that rarely gets reported in the media. Most everyone is familiar with the type of aliens known as the Greys—the large, oblong-headed creatures with the oversized, almond-shaped black eyes that seem to appear on everything Hollywood makes. But if you delve a bit outside of the mainstream alien reports, you start to discover that a lot of weird creatures are thought to be visiting us. I am leaving the question of whether or not eyewitnesses have the same imagination or that truly weird beings are visiting us up to you to decide.

History of Lore:

Throughout the history of UFO reports, seeing a tin can shaped object was not as rare as one might think. The fact is, though, that most of the reports claim that the UFO itself was shaped like a tin can, rather than the creatures inside. It is extremely difficult to find cases similar to this one, where the creatures were so oddly-shaped. There are numerous cases that involve strange creatures descending from UFOs—some are shaped like robots and some have multiple appendages, while some even tend to resemble us—yet none hold any of the same characteristics as the Long Prairie tri-pod tin cans. Having no previous data to fall back on, we are forced to take this case on its own merits...no matter how bizarre it may seem.

Investigation Log:

On October 23, 1965, 19-year-old radio announcer James Townsend was driving west along Highway 27 from Little Falls to Long Prairie when his life took a drastic change for the weird. Four miles outside of Long Prairie, a quick check of his watch showed it was 7:15 pm. As he rounded a curve in the road, he spotted a 30-to-40-foot rocket-like object straddling the pavement ahead of him. Townsend told the *St. Paul Pioneer Press*, "my car engine, lights, and radio went out and I slammed on my brakes," coming to a halt 20 feet from the craft. His first thought was to ram the craft with his vehicle in hopes of knocking it over and securing proof of its existence, but with a dead car that plan was quickly discarded. Thinking that he could simply walk over and topple the object by hand, Townsend bravely exited his car and started walking toward the craft. "When I got to the front of my car three creatures that looked like individual tin cans on tripods, and were about six inches tall, came from behind the rocket," he stated.

Amazed by what he was seeing, Townsend noted that the creatures had no visible eyes…yet he somehow got the impression that they had no problem seeing him. With the bizarre creatures now directly in front on him, he had no desire to pursue his plan of tipping over the craft. Instead, he just stood motionless, staring at the creatures for what seemed "like ages." (Later Townsend would estimate the time at about 3 minutes). The creatures made no attempt to communicate with him, and he took notice that the whole area seemed engulfed in eerie silence. As the creatures retreated back to their rocket, a bright colorless light began glowing at the bottom of the craft and with a loud hum breaking the quiet, the rocket took off into the sky. When the rocket reached about a quarter mile, the bottom light shut off and the craft disappeared into the sky. As soon as the craft exited from sight, the power to Townsend's car returned and his engine, lights, and radio started back up on their own.

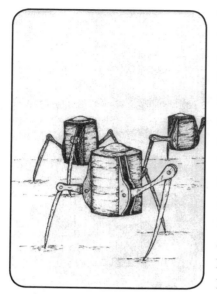

Odd looking creatures that Townsend encountered

With his heart pounding and "legs like rubber," Townsend speed off at 90 mph to Long Prairie to report his sighting— the whole time wondering if anyone would believe his odd story. His first stop was at the Todd County Sheriff's office. He was greeted by Sheriff Jim Bain and Deputy Lavern Lubitz, who listened intently as he spilled out the details of his otherworldly encounter. Intrigued by the amazing story, the law enforcers convinced a hesitant and shaken Townsend to take them out to the exact spot of the sighting. At the site, surrounded by rolling green grasses, the men failed to find any remnants of the mysterious rocket craft. Even without finding evidence of the craft, the group did discover the alleged landing site wet with three strips of oil-like substance which ran parallel with the road, each about a yard long and spaced four inches apart. The finding was odd enough to cause Deputy Lubitz to tell the *St. Paul Pioneer Press*, "I don't know what they were but I've looked at a lot of roads and never saw anything like them before." If any samples of the mysterious substance were taken, it was not reported in an official capacity. In his book, *Oddball Minnesota*, author Jerome Pohlen claimed that shortly after Townsend's sighting, a highway crew came out and replaced the section of road where the incident took place, leading some to suspect that perhaps an alien craft did land out on Highway 27, and the Government acted swiftly to cover up any possible evidence.

Skeptics point out that if indeed a 30-40-foot rocket was flying around the area, surely someone other than Townsend would have witnessed it too…which is exactly what happened. Word quickly spread of Townsend's sighting, and before long other strange reports were pouring in from the entire region. The *Long Prairie Leader* printed several of these eyewitness accounts that seem to corroborate his sighting. The first one took place on Saturday evening to a group of men who, while out hunting, noticed a strong light shining down on them from above. This apparently disembodied light was so powerful that it lit up the ground around them as though it was daytime. The light was so intense that nothing outside of the light could be seen in the sky. Another separate group of hunters also spotted a "lighted object circle around and around their farm," and again all attempts to locate the source of the light failed. Later that very same evening, three Sauk Rapids residents were traveling home from Milaca around 9:15 pm when they reported seeing an unidentified object in the sky. "It appeared as a bright light, shaded from orange to white in color," they stated. We couldn't distinguish a shape, just a bright light." According to the Sheriff's Department, numerous other witnesses who wished to remain nameless also called in with the UFO sightings. Whatever was responsible for these multiple sightings seemed to be flying low, because witnesses reported that the light would often get blocked out by nearby trees.

One of the many newspaper headlines that
featured the baffling story

This case was investigated by noted Project Blue Book researcher Dr. J. Allen Hynek, who included it in his 1971 book, *The Hynek UFO Report*. Hynek spoke with both Townsend and Sheriff Bain and took up the case on his own when Project Blue Book simply closed the case with no official investigation—they viewed any case involving possible alien life forms too wacky to possibly be true. Hynek noted that the case featured a common element shared with other CE-IIIs (Close Encounter of the Third Kind – sighting of occupant(s) takes place, but no interaction between occupants and witnesses occur), writing, "The reported 'creatures' generally climb aboard and take off without seeming to desire communication." Adding further credibility to this case, Hynek wrote, "One would think that if all these cases were hoaxes, imaginative and detailed descriptions of the 'creatures' would be even more bizarre than Mr. T---------." (Hynek did not include Townsend's name in the case).

With such a bizarre case it would be easy for those involved to brush it off as nonsense, but contrary to this, both the sheriff and deputy believed that Townsend was telling them the truth. The Sheriff went out of his way in vouching for Townsend, saying that he personally knew him and believed him to be "reliable and level-headed." Townsend himself was considered to have upstanding character within the community, didn't drink, and attended church regularly.

In my investigation into this case, I stopped in at the Morrison County Records Department to try to locate the original police report, only to be told that the file had been thrown out many, many years ago. So much time had passed since the sighting that, outside of the copious newspaper stories, little else of evidence was left. Asking around town, I discovered that both of the law officers that investigated the case were deceased. I also learned that Townsend had moved away from the area years ago and had gotten tired of talking about his sighting and wished that it had never happened to him. With little else to go on, I decided to venture out to the approximate area of the sighting to get a feel of what transpired so many years ago. Paralleled by rolling hills and forests, the road still projects a rural eeriness to it, even though it is only four miles from Long Prairie. After driving back and forth along Hwy 27, I pulled off onto a desolate side road, got out of my car and patiently sat on the roof watching the sky and road for the rocket ship. As the hours passed by, I couldn't help but wonder as to the origin and purpose of the mysterious Long Prairie visitors. Was it truly a genuine case of extraterrestrial visitation? A hallucination? A hoax? Or did Townsend simply misidentify a more natural man-made object? Perhaps we may never know. Townsend himself believed that the rocket and its occupants were "an exploratory ship from space, here to look us over," telling the *St. Paul Pioneer Press*, "I was sure of two things—the rocket was a spaceship of some kind and the three objects that came out of it were creatures like nothing else in the animal world." In a fitting end to the interview, Townsend claimed, "this scared me like I've never been scared before."

The Willow River Beast(s)

Where To Encounter It:

Willow River, MN
Forested areas that surround the area.

Directions:

Your best chance of seeing a creature is to explore any of the numerous forested areas and small lakes that dot the countryside of Willow River.

Creature Lore:

The Bigfoot field of study is filled with thousands of credible sightings from all over the world, some of which date back hundreds of years. With the combination of early newspaper accounts, files from researchers, and internet databases, a large number of Bigfoot sightings have been complied. With this expansive list of sightings, we are able to pin down many common factors that occur during a sighting. One interesting aspect of the sightings is that the majority of witnesses report seeing a singular creature. If we assume that these creatures are flesh and blood beings (which some researchers do not), then it logically follows that there must be a sufficient number of these creatures around to keep the species from dying out. If these creatures do indeed travel in mating pairs or packs, they are rarely spotted that way. It is much rarer for witnesses to see multiple creatures, especially ones of varying heights or perceived gender roles. The rarity of such multiple sightings is what makes this forthcoming case so intriguing.

History of Lore:

As is the case with so many other rural communities, it is very difficult to begin to develop a history of sightings in the small, tight-lipped city of Willow River.

The *Minnesota Bigfoot* website contains an interesting sighting that occurred in 1978 in the small town of Hugo, Minnesota (one hour and fifteen minutes north of Willow River). Three young friends spent many of their afternoons out hunting in the nearby woods. During several of their hunts, they discovered large, freshly-made footprints that they attributed to a bear. One winter day, they stumbled into a big open clearing. Standing at the far edge of the field were two Bigfoot-looking creatures with their backs to the kids. Amazed that they had apparently snuck up on the creatures without being noticed, the friends stared in awe at the mysterious beings directly in front of them. Immediately, the friends noticed that the two creatures were of different size. While both creatures had large, stocky frames, the bigger of the two looked to be over 7 feet tall, with its companion about a foot shorter. The witness believed that perhaps the smaller creature was a female or younger Bigfoot. Interestingly, the medium brown fur that ran the length of both their bodies also completely covered their faces as well. The witnesses described the hair/fur as being the same length as that of a grizzly bear. Then, as if on cue, the startled creatures turned around and looked directly at the terrified young men who thought better of sticking around and tore off for the safety of their home. I was fascinated with this case, because it contains several rare physical characteristics which you are about to read.

Investigation Log:

Back during the summer of 1972, Dennis Murphy was in Willow River to do some fishing on one of its many secluded lakes. He was cruising down a lonely gravel road, when up ahead to his right he spotted two white figures standing together in a small open field. Murphy got the feeling that they also had spotted him and rather than retreat into the woods, they froze in place hoping that the vehicle would pass by without noticing them. He slowed down a bit, careful not to skid his tires on the gravel and risk further spooking the creatures. There, standing off in the distance, were two Bigfoot creatures of different sizes poised side by side one another. Then, within fifty yards of the beasts, he noticed that the big one, which he assumed was the male, looked to be well over eight feet tall, had extremely broad shoulders and was covered in white fur. The smaller, and presumably female, beast looked to be around 4-5 feet tall and was also covered in long, thick, white fur—the only difference being that the female's face was entirely covered by her fur. As Murphy stared in disbelief, he got the sense that the large creature was staring right back at him with a look that said you better not stop here—a warning that Murphy took seriously as he keep on his route. A few moments later, he garnered up his courage, swung back, and got out to explore the then empty site. Amazed that the creatures could have covered the distance of the field in such a short period of time, Murphy left with more questions than answers, leading him on a life-long search for the truth behind Bigfoot.

A thick forest in Willow River

Back in February of 2004, I interviewed Dennis Murphy on both my local TV and radio shows out of Eau Claire, Wisconsin. He brought a truckload of equipment that he uses on his investigations, along with several plaster casts of footprints and a few photographs of the alleged beast. I was immediately struck with his sincerity as he retold his 1972 encounter. Murphy seemed to be a man on a forty-year quest to get answers regarding the bizarre creatures he spotted back in Willow River. In 2002, Murphy's patience and thorough research put him back face to face with another similar creature…this time the encounter took place in the heart of a Wisconsin forest (I covered this case in my book, *The Wisconsin Road Guide to Mysterious Creatures*).

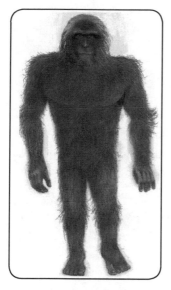

Drawing of what Dennis Murphy spotted in the woods.

Willow River prides itself on being a true haven for outdoor enthusiasts. With plenty of secluded lakes, thick forests and miles of recreation trails, Willow River allows residents and visitors to become one with their surroundings. That is exactly what a local family had in mind when they set off on their ATVs to do some partridge hunting in the fall of 2007. It was around 5:30 in the evening and the family had just succeeded in scaring up some birds, so they turned off their vehicles and waited as the husband started to walk a loop to try and get a shot at the birds. As he was walking along, a large Bigfoot creature jumped out of nowhere and started running back in the direction of where the wife and kids were positioned. Turning to get a better look, the husband was able to catch a glimpse of the creature's back as it ran within 25 feet of the rest of the family. As it rushed by the startled family, the weight of the beast was so great that its footfalls could be heard as its lumbering feet crashed to the ground. With a cone-shaped head and long, ape-like arms, the beast moved surprisingly fast for a creature of its immense

61

size. The family noted that while it ran, its palms were faced backwards as its long arms swung at its side. The case was first reported to Bob Olson of the Northern Minnesota Bigfoot Research Team. Olson had initially interviewed the woman and, impressed with her sincerity, he deemed it a credible case. Eager for any new details, he gave me the contact information of the witnesses. When I spoke with them, they quickly informed me that they did not want to discuss their sighting. After interviewing a couple thousand witnesses, it becomes easier to "feel out" witnesses to better gauge where they are at with their experience. One can usually tell those who view their experience through skeptical eyes versus the true believers, the shy vs. the outgoing, and the curious vs. the frightened. What I was picking up on with the Willow River case were witnesses who were struggling to come to grips with what transpired out in the woods. Regardless of the phenomenon, there is no overriding method in which witnesses deal with their experiences. Some, like Dennis Murphy, become fascinated with the subject and seek to discover answers; others tend to push their experience as far away from their memory as possible. I roamed around the small city of Willow River, speaking to several residents about the topic of Bigfoot and discovered that many scoffed at the idea of taking such reports seriously. After spending only a couple of hours talking with intensely skeptical individuals around town, I found myself sympathizing with witnesses who are reluctant to share their story out of fear of being ridiculed in such a small social circles. Perhaps the human fear of being ostracized by one's community is a undiscovered creature's best friend.

One of the many area lakes that could provide habitat for an unknown creature

As with most of the cases in this guide, there are no concrete answers to be found. Contrary to what some researchers like to claim, those in the field are left with many unanswered questions that have been raised for centuries. Is it possible that the young hunters in Hugo caught a glimpse of the very same pair of creatures that Murphy saw in Willow River six years prior? If so, are those creatures still in the area? Are they even still alive? Or have they migrated, been killed, or simply died of old age? With no answers, the mysterious sightings in Willow Creek may never be solved or even solvable for that matter, but luckily for us there are people out there like Dennis Murphy who will give it one hell of a try.

The Floodwood Bigfoot

Where To Encounter It:

Floodwood, MN

Directions:

From Floodwood, head north on County Highway 73 and you will be in the area where most of the sightings occur.

Creature Lore:

When asked to make a mental picture of Bigfoot most people think of what is shown in the famous Patterson Bigfoot video. They tend to think of an extremely tall ape-looking creature covered from head to toe in thick, dark fur as it walks effortlessly on its hind legs. Although this is by far the most commonly reported description of Bigfoot, many in the general public are unaware as to just how diverse and varying reports of Bigfoot really are. By most accounts, the creatures are unusually tall, their height ranging from seven feet all the way up to over 10 feet, but this is not always the case, as evidenced here. Researchers tend to speculate that the more human-sized beings could possibly be the females of the species or even young offspring. Even the color of its hair varies widely from sighting to sighting and location to location. Most reports detail long, thick, matted down, reddish-brown, auburn or black hair, although reports of beige, white, or silver colored hair have also been filed. One common physical description that arrives from sightings is that—regardless of their size, shape, or color—Bigfoot creatures are almost always described as walking or running on their hind legs, leading many to classify it as a biped.

History of Lore:

While exploring the area, the first thing one notices is the sheer amount of forest and thick brush that engulfs the entire region. This is the scene that comes to mind when people think of the Northwoods of Minnesota. It doesn't take a huge imagination to believe that something unknown could live undiscovered among the forest. Like many rural towns, the residents of Floodwood tend to keep tales that do not easily fit into polite conversation to themselves—yet there have always been vague accounts of local

Bigfoot sightings devoid of any specific details so as not to be attributed to any one individual. This self-imposed gag order on talking about anything paranormal or strange was broken in 1968 with Uno Heilklila's bizarre sighting. Even his sighting did little to break the cycle of secrecy when it came to talking with strangers and visitors about odd sightings, leaving us with only mere speculation when wondering just how many Floodwood Bigfoot sightings have gone unreported.

Investigation Log:

In 1968, Uno Heikkila was out hunting in the thick forests about 10 miles north of Floodwood when he witnessed something so strange that it compelled him to write a letter detailing his experience to Roger Patterson (from the infamous Patterson Bigfoot footage). According to Heikkila, he was out hunting and was perched out on a stump watching for the slightest movement among the dense brush, when about 125 feet away something up in a tree caught his eye. As he remained still, Heikkila watched as a four-and-a-half-foot non-human Bigfoot creature jumped to the ground from its hiding spot 25 feet up on the tree. Much to his surprise, the creature walked out of sight on its back feet. For reasons not stated, he did not follow after the diminutive creature. Based on my further research, the sighting was not covered by any local media and only got a short summary in John Green's *The Sasquatch File*. Roger Patterson's book *Do Abominable Snowmen of America Really Exist?* was released in 1966 and therefore did not contain the Heikkila's 1968 sighting.

Road where the small Bigfoot was spotted

What originally caught my attention about this case is the uncanny resemblance of this creature to that of a similar looking creature Dennis Murphy spotted only one hour away from Floodwood (see The Willow River Beast) four years after Heikkila's spotting. Witnesses who report seeing smaller sized Bigfoot creatures are in the minority. Only a small fraction of reports tell of a short or smaller Bigfoot, making these accounts relatively rare when compared with their full-sized counterparts. Needless to say, when I discovered that two people had reported seeing a half-sized Bigfoot creature within a few miles and a few years of each other, it really piqued my interest.

Upon my initial visit to Floodwood, I had concluded that Heikkila was the only one who had a sighting in the area, and outside of writing to Patterson he had kept the story to himself in fear of what others might think. Being that the sighting was over 40 years old, I was unable to track down Heikkila to ascertain any additional details of his story. My first stop was at the Minnesota DNR Forestry Station. Based on their close dealing with hunters, snowmobilers, hikers, and the like, I figured that they may have come across some stories of Bigfoot in the area. However, the ranger informed me that he was not familiar with any strange creature reports from the area. The ranger did tell me that there were several bears in the area, and he had just seen one a day earlier. Maybe Heikkila had actually spooked a small bear from the tree rather than a Bigfoot. Yet, in my hundreds of talks with game and wildlife experts over the years, they have all assured me that it would be highly unlikely for a bear to stand on its hind legs for any substantial length of time— especially if had been scared and wanted to make a fast escape.

The area is surrounded with open fields and lush forests

Leaving the forestry station, I spent the better part of an afternoon scouring the general area of Heikkila's sighting (10 miles north of Floodwood) searching for signs of Bigfoot and again I was surprised at the amount of undeveloped land that was in the area. On numerous occasions I have been on research expeditions in huge forests and rainforests that dwarfed the area around Floodwood, but something about the land lead me to feel as though it was much larger and remote than it actually was. Having little more than mosquito bites to show for my search, I headed back into town with hopes of finding other witnesses.

Does this creature continue to lurk in Floodwood?

My last stop was at the local newspaper. Over the years, I have found that local newspapers are often a wealth of information on local history, folklore, and weird goings on. I spoke at length with the editor, who had an interest in the Bigfoot topic and was able to steer me towards several witnesses in the area who have seen something strange in their forests. The editor was so convinced that some large bipeds inhabited the area that he often left food out in his backyard, in hopes of enticing the Bigfoot creature. And even though the editor was willing to speak with me about Bigfoot, the other witnesses were not. Even when promised that their names would remain confidential and not appear in this guide, they declined to re-visit their sightings, thereby adding more cases to the ever growing number of sightings which go unreported.

Rochester Bigfoot

Where To Encounter It:

1969 Sighting- Highway 52

1979 Sighting- Between Marvale Ave. and Rose Haven Additions

Directions:

1969 sighting – Head south out of town on Highway 52 for a few miles and you will be in the area of the sighting.

1979 sighting – The exact location of the encounter is unknown. If you take Highway 36 (Marion Rd. SE) south to the area between Marvale Ave. SE and Pearl Court SE you will be in the area of the sighting.

Creature Lore:

One of the most intriguing aspects of Bigfoot research is the sheer unpredictability of the sightings. It seems as though there is no rhyme or reason to the various encounters with regard to time, season, and location. Although the majority of the encounters occur during the daylight hours, many sightings of the mysterious creature have taken place at all times of both day and night. Likewise, the creature doesn't seem to abide by any human calendar, as evidenced by the numerous sightings that take place during the winter months, poking a hole in the theory that perhaps these creatures like to hibernate through the winter. We also tend to believe that, like all other wild creatures, Bigfoot would need a habitat where food was plentiful, where water was easily accessible, and an area that contained enough cover to ensure its privacy. Even when we take all of the above-mentioned variables into account, the act of encountering a Bigfoot seems all but random, which is exactly what transpired on the outskirts of Rochester.

History of Lore:

We tend to believe that Bigfoot sightings only take place in the densely forested areas of the Northwoods of MN, and we don't often associate bustling cities like Rochester as being a hotbed of paranormal activity. The city of Rochester is a bit deceiving... at first glance you assume it is a large metropolitan city, yet if you travel a few miles from downtown, the area quickly turns rural. Littered with plenty of forests, rivers, farms, and livestock the place becomes fertile grounds for Bigfoot sightings. Research shows that the majority of paranormal sightings are never reported; people either don't know who to report their sighting to or, more commonly, they are afraid of what others may think of them, causing many interesting cases to go undocumented. With such a low rate of reporting, it is difficult to determine just how far back the Bigfoot sightings of the area date.

Investigation Log:

Busy highway where creature was seen

The July 1969 edition of *SAGA Magazine* reported the startling story of a young Iowa student who witnessed something very strange on the outskirts of Rochester. According to the article, sometime in spring of '69 Larry Hawkins was heading south on Highway 52 as he made his way to Decorah, Iowa. It was nearing midnight when, just a few miles south of town, his headlights flashed across an outline of a figure crouched beside the road. Thinking that any person out at such an hour had to be in trouble, Hawkins "braked down and pulled onto the shoulder" of the road to assist with the situation. As he came to a stop, Hawkins quickly realized that the figure crouching alongside the highway was certainly not human. Instead, what he spotted was a creature "ape-like in appearance with thick shoulders" that was fully covered with thick dense hair. Immediately, the lurking creature leaped from its crouching position and darted off up a steep hill that led to the woods. Bravely, Hawkins exited his car and walked over to where the beast had been. There Hawkins discovered that the beast had been crouching over the remains of a dead rabbit. Looking over the carcass, Hawkins was unable to find any blood on the hide, leading him to believe that the rabbit had been road kill and not torn apart by the creature's teeth. During his examination of the rabbit, the night air was pierced by a thunderous roar that rang out from the thick woods where the creature had run off. The terrifying howl spooked Hawkins, and with his nerves starting to peak, he quickly made his way back to the car and sped off. He stated, "I didn't stop until I got to a police station." Due to the bizarre nature and late hour of the report, the officers on duty erroneously assumed that the whole thing was some sort of practical joke. Instead of investigating the sighting, they accused Hawkins of being drunk—an accusation that left Hawkins angry and bitter about even trying to make the report.

The highway would provide a lot of road kill animals

One aspect of this case that I find fascinating is that it included the spotting of killed prey or road kill along with the sighting of the creature. Researchers have long speculated on the possible eating habits of these Bigfoot creatures. I do have a handful of other cases where these creatures have been seen with small game carcasses. In 2000, I investigated a case near Neillsville, Wisconsin where a local man (James Hughes) came upon a Bigfoot crossing the road while carrying a carcass of a small deer or goat in its hand. Mr. Hughes told me that he was unable to positively identify the dead animal, due to the fact that he could not break his gaze from the terrifying eyes of the Bigfoot. In her book, *The Beast of Bray Road,* paranormal researcher Linda Godfrey wrote of several cases where witnesses spied an unknown beast in the process of inspecting/ eating/carrying a dead animal carcass. In addition to the sightings of Bigfoot consuming fruits and plants, there are now enough good cases out there that we can postulate that the Bigfoot is probably an omnivore, taking prey either by hunting or by being opportunistic of freshly-killed roadside animals.

Area where Bigfoot appeared to a mother and her children

As much as Hawkins was ridiculed by the police, it may provide him some comfort to know that whatever the creature was that he encountered, he wouldn't be the only one who would encounter it. On the evening of Friday, December 14, 1979, a young woman was traveling the road between the Rose Haven and Marvale additions of Rochester when her headlights flashed across some type of creature she had never seen before. The very next morning the frightened woman walked into the Olmstad County Sheriff's office and recounted her story. According to the *Rochester Post-Bulletin,* the woman was driving home with her two children, ages 2 and 3, when her headlights "picked up a huge beast." The woman described the enormous creature as being over 7 feet tall and estimated its weight somewhere between 250-300 pounds. The woman could make out the facial features of the beast and stated that it had "a huge mouth with a pig-like nose" that appeared to be "very ugly."

Interestingly, the woman reported that when hit by the beams of her headlights, the creature "attempted to cover its eye from the glare," at which point the woman noticed that the creature's arm "did not bend like a normal arm." The manner in which the creature did bend its arm was never reported. The woman refused to give the officers her name for fear that her friends and neighbors would think she had gone crazy. Fearing criticism, the woman initially wasn't even going to report the incident, but changed her mind because she felt it would "allay the fears of her children" who were pretty shaken up by the event. The woman was adamant that whatever she saw "it was definitely not a man." Just to be on the safe side, the Sheriff's office sent out a couple of deputies to check the area but "could find no trace or tracks of the creature."

Newspaper headline on the mysterious sighting

Researching this case turned out to be a lot more difficult than it should have been. First, as mentioned, the woman refused to divulge her name, making her report completely anonymous, and making her nearly impossible to track down. Without the witness, my next step was to find the original police report, so I headed over to the Olmstad County Sheriff's office only to discover that unless a case involved a major crime like murder, the department only kept it on file for seven years. With no witness name and no police file, I looked to track down the reporter who had written the article, hoping that he might recall some additional details that did not make it to print. Once again, bad luck seemed to plague this case when I discovered that the reporter had recently passed away. A bit disheartened, I headed out to the area of the sighting hoping to find something that would add to this case. I ended up speaking with several long-time residents of the Marvale additions who were unaware of the beast seen in 1979 and had also not heard of any recent sightings in the area. This case was quickly barreling toward a dead end. Unable to gather up any additional information on this case, I was left with more questions than answers. I can only hope that future witnesses will follow in the footsteps of Larry Hawkins and the unidentified woman so that we may one day get to the bottom of this Bigfoot mystery.

The secluded area where the Bigfoot was spotted

Bigfoot of Deer River

Where To Encounter It:

Deer River Area

Directions:

This is the one case from this guide where I am including a general area rather than a specific place. The reason for this is due to the numerous sightings all over the region ranging from tracks found at Six Mile Lake Road in Bena to the hotly debated Bigfoot photo captured in Remer.

Your best chance of sighting a Bigfoot is to travel the back roads of the region.

To report a sighting contact the Northern Minnesota Bigfoot Research Team at 218-246-2150

Creature Lore:

When most people hear of a Bigfoot sighting they tend to think of the expansive forests of Oregon or California which are home to many Bigfoot encounters. Yet all throughout the small towns of Minnesota's Northwoods a mysterious Bigfoot creature has been spotted so many times that it is started to give the western states a run for their money. When it comes to why a certain area becomes a hotbed for sightings, no concrete answers are available. Some researchers theorize that Bigfoot creatures are migratory animals that follow some unknown travel route as they make their way across the country. Contrasting this theory is the belief that these creatures tend to bunker down in an area where they have found it to their liking. If the Bigfoot is indeed a flesh and blood creature or animal then it would need an area that could provide cover, possess an adequate amount of food and water supply, and have enough other Bigfoot creatures for the possibility of mating, all of which appear to be plenty abundant in the Northwoods.

History of Lore:

The northern forests of Minnesota have long been seen as a mysterious place. Native Americans of the area believed whole-heartedly that Sasquatch lived throughout the forests. Tales of these Sasquatch creatures differed from those of the Wendigo, and are often viewed as being supernatural in origin. Some of the most bizarre tales come from the old-timers who told me that while participating in drumming circles they would feel Bigfoot creatures gather barely outside of where they could be spotted, as though they knew the range of human sight.

In his book, *The M-Files*, author Jay Rath tells of 1911 encounter where two northern Minnesota hunters followed a pair of odd looking footprints that eventually led them to a human giant "with long arms and short dark hair on its body." What the two hunters did after encountering the giant is unknown.

Investigation Log:

In 2006, infamous Bigfoot researcher (and repeat hoaxer) Tom Biscardi brought his film crew to Deer River in search of the much reported Bigfoot. Biscardi interviewed several eyewitnesses for his documentary movie *Bigfoot Lives*. Outside of collecting some interesting stories and "finding" some footprints, Biscardi left the area empty handed.

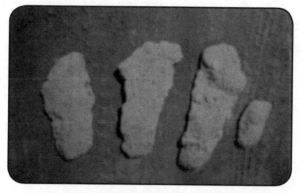

A few of Bob Olson's large footprint casts

Having heard a lot about the Northwoods sightings I headed off to Deer River to pay a visit to researcher Bob Olson, who along with Donald Sherman, founded the Northern Minnesota Bigfoot Research Team. Over the last five years Olson has collected over 50 Bigfoot sightings throughout the area. Olson has also discovered dozens of extremely large footprints alongside of Six Mile Lake Road, the casts of which he proudly displays at his place of business. As a life-long resident of the area Olson had gained the trust of those living in the area enabling him to document encounters that witnesses would not have felt comfortable telling to a stranger.

Bob Olson displays several enormous footprint casts

Olson shared with me a couple of very interesting sightings from the area. One case was that of a woman who was out driving near the town of Bena when she spotted something walking along a set of railroad tracks. Grabbing a closer look the woman could now see that it was a Bigfoot creature that appeared to be staring right at her. The strange encounter was so intense that the woman broke down into tears and claimed that the creature had looked right into her soul.

Another short sighting occurred in 2006, after a woman was returning home from an evening at the Deer River Casino. The woman was driving along Highway 2 just west of Ball Club when a small Bigfoot like creature popped out of a swampy area, looked at the driver, and then quickly retreated back into the swamp. Although the woman only got a quick glance at the creature, she was convinced it was a Bigfoot, and she wasn't the only one to spot it as according to the *Cass Lake Times* at approximately the same time of the above sighting Kit Blum had just left his father's house and was heading home to Deer River when something flashed in front of his headlights. Catching a good look at the beast Blum noted that it was unlike anything he had ever seen before. Moving across the road was a strange creature with a hairless dark grey shiny wax-like face that was offset by a small nose and human looking lips. Blum watched as the beast swung its arms rapidly while passing by before disappearing into Lake Lillian. After receiving the report, the Northern Minnesota Bigfoot Research

Team spoke with Blum and also investigated the area of the sighting where they discovered a mangled deer carcass lodged in a very high up tree branch leading the researchers to believe that it wasn't put there by any normal animal.

The entire region is rife with Bigfoot reports

In talking with Olson I was amazed at his dedication to the search of the elusive creature. Pulling out case after case of field reports, dozens of plaster casts, and maps marking most of the recent sightings, Olson had certainly done his home work. Such was his interest in the field that if news broke today that Olson had captured indisputable evidence of Bigfoot I would not be surprised in the least.

But not everyone in Deer River is a believer of Bigfoot as noted by the *Cass Lake Times* which interviewed Keith Matson, a retired US Forest Service Inventory Technician, who spent 28 years working in forests of the Northwoods and believes that "there is no evidence to support the believer's claims."

In 2009, Tim Kedrowski and his sons, Peter and Casey, captured a photo of a mysterious creature on a game trail camera that had been set up on their hunting land in Remer. The photo purportedly shows a large hairy ape-like beast walking upright through the woods during the evening. The photo has caused quite a bit of disagreement among researchers who continue to try to prove or disprove it.

Many of the footprints have been discovered alongside the back roads

Each year dozens of credible sightings are added to the lengthy list of northern Minnesota Bigfoot encounters. Many of these sightings garner wide media attention which in turn generates interest among residents who keep a more watchful eye as they move through their day. With so many people on the lookout, it may just be a matter of time before someone finally solves the mystery of the Deer River Bigfoot.

Coon Rapids Kangaroos

Where To Encounter It:

Highway 10 & Anoka County Fairgrounds
Coon Rapids, MN

Directions:

Highway 10 – Most of the sightings took place near this main highway through Coon Rapids.

Anoka County Fairgrounds – Take Highway 47 to the north. When you pass the fairgrounds, head west for approximately 1 mile and you will be in the area of the 1967 sighting.

Creature Lore:

Thanks to the wonderful job of Australia's tourism department, there is hardly anyone who doesn't associate the oddly adorable kangaroo with the Land Down Under. For the most part it would seem that kangaroos like their homeland, because they are not indigenous to any other part of the world. So why is it that the marsupial has been popping up around American cities for nearly 100 years? Animals that appear in places where they are not known to inhabit are usually referred to as out-of-place animals. In Europe they have a similar problem with "ABCs" (Alien Big Cats) showing up where they are not supposed to be living. Here in the Midwest the most commonly reported out-of-place animal is the cougar, which we have been told is no longer living in these parts. Each year, however, hundreds of witnesses see them, their tracks can be found all over, and several have even been killed. Obviously, animals rarely abide by the geographic limitations of where humans think they should be.

With out-of-place kangaroos it gets a bit tricky in that not only are they being sighted, they also display an uncanny ability to avoiding capture. Hundreds of witnesses have encountered these hopping transplants, hundreds of search parties have been sent after them, yet they are rarely ever captured. Where do these creatures go? That is the question that the residents of Coon Rapids have been asking themselves for over fifty years.

History of Lore:

In 1934, a deadly animal was stalking residents of the small Tennessee town of South Pittsburgh. Labeled as a kangaroo by witnesses, the creature exhibited all the main characteristics of a mountain lion. Residents were on edge at the discovery of numerous dogs, including several German Shepherd police dogs, torn apart by the unidentified killer animal. Concern over the kangaroo only grew from the growing list of sheep and cattle that were also being devoured during all hours of the night. Officials tried pinning the gruesome killings on a mountain lion that had been recently killed on a nearby ridge. Still, the animal deaths did not cease. The *Ludington Daily News* reported that a "farmer in the Battle Creek section of the county reported several sheep were killed by the animal several days after the lynx was slain." One witness, Rev. W.J. Hancock, had his story quoted in the *Hutchinson News.* "It was as fast as lighting and looked like a giant kangaroo running and leaping." Residents also continued to see the kangaroo after the alleged culprit (mountain lion) had been killed. The newspaper further reported that the "fear of the 'kangaroo' still exists and many go about armed after nightfall."

In August of 1965, central Kansas found itself in the midst of a full-blown kangaroo mystery. For several weeks witnesses had been reporting the appearance of a kangaroo popping up all over the region. The out-of- place kangaroo was first seen west of Junction City along the busy Interstate 70. Four students at Kansas City State were driving home one evening when they saw the kangaroo once again sitting on the edge of a highway east of Wakefield. The *Salina Journal* covered the story, claiming the young men "first thought it was a coyote...by the time they stopped and turned their car to shine its headlights on the animal it had disappeared." One of the many explanations for the wayward kangaroo was that it was an escapee from a small circus that had been performing in that area a few weeks prior to all of the sightings.

The Windy City also got in on the kangaroo action when a vanishing kangaroo in Chicago eluded capture in 1975. One year later and a few hours west, the town of Rock Island, Illinois, was also visited by a vanishing kangaroo. On an early April morning the local police dispatcher received an excited call from Harry Masterson, a transportation rate clerk, who was out walking his dog about 6:30 am when he noticed a 3-foot-tall kangaroo hop over the hill across the street. The *Cedar Rapids Gazette* wrote that Masterson stated that the creature was "either a kangaroo or a wallaby—they look a lot alike." A squad car that was dispatched to the area of the sighting came up empty in its kangaroo hunt.

In 1978, the people of Wisconsin found themselves seemingly overrun with kangaroo sightings. In his book, *The W-Files*, author Jay Rath documents kangaroo sightings coming in from the cities of Waukesha, Pewaukee, Eau Claire, Brookfield, and others. In Menomonee Falls, two 23-year-old men saw a similar kangaroo creature lurking off of the side of the road and were able to snap off two pictures of it on their Polaroid camera. One of the photos shows what appears to be a tan animal with matching physical characteristics to that of a wallaby or kangaroo.

Investigation Log:

When faced with a paranormal experience many people struggle to find some outlet where they can report their sighting. Usually this means that reports get funneled to the police, newspapers, TV stations, DNR officials, etc. Often these claims go unnoticed by paranormal investigators and fade into oblivion as official files are thrown out, burned, or simply lost. Sometimes a researcher will get lucky and happen to get a case that would normally slip through the cracks. For the Coon Rapids kangaroos, that researcher happened to be Loren Coleman, a noted cryptozoologist, who fortunately documented these bizarre sightings and chronicled them in his 2001 book, *Mysterious America*.

Anoka County Fairgrounds

Coleman wrote that back in 1957, two young brothers, seven and nine, were busy playing in a heavily wooded area just off of Highway 10 in Coon Rapids. Thinking that they were alone in the woods, the boys were surprised to see two kangaroos hopping side by side through the woods. The boys watched in awe as the five-foot beasts hopped out of the woods into a nearby clearing before disappearing into another heavily wooded area. Being that the kangaroos were hopping less than 50 feet from the boys, they were easily able to see that the creatures' fur was light tan to medium brown in color. Upon hearing of her sons' encounter, Mrs. Barbara Battmer began discussing the case, which led to more witnesses coming forward. Whatever type of animal these creatures were, one thing was certain—they were not leaving anytime soon. They were spotted again in 1957, and in 1958 another set of brothers came home shouting about seeing an enormous rabbit as big as they were hopping around the woods.

Mr. and Mrs. Willard Hayes reported to Coleman that on the evening of April 24, 1967, they spotted what looked like two oversized bunnies standing in an open field near the Anoka County Fairgrounds. Interestingly, a few weeks later in May of 1967, the *Anoka County Union* carried a story outlining the concerns of local residents over the amount of dogs that were running wild throughout the county. Although it is highly unlikely for witnesses to mistake a stray dog for a 5-foot kangaroo, the timing of the two events warrants some consideration.

Author Jay Rath set out to find the kangaroo witnesses while researching his book, *M-Files,* writing that his efforts proved to be futile when he was unable to locate them. Being that the original sightings occurred over 60 years ago, the chances of finding the witnesses remained unlikely. With the slim possibility of locating the whereabouts of the witnesses, I stopped into the Anoka County Historical Society Museum in Anoka and began searching through the old phone books hoping to dig up a phone number or even an address. After several hours of scouring through phone books, newspaper archives, and death records, I was only able to obtain information on the 1967 witnesses, Mr. and Mrs. Hayes, whom I discovered were both deceased. When it came to the other witnesses, I came up empty-handed too.

Touring the area of the sightings today, it is difficult to imagine the surroundings as they were back in the 1950s and 60s. Packed with homes, businesses, and general sprawl, the area loses some of the secluded ambiance that must have engrossed it back during the sightings. Still, even with the changes, there is enough wild countryside left to provide shelter to any out-of-place creature looking to remain hidden for another 60 years.

Area where two of the kangaroos were spotted

Explanations for these seemingly out-of-place creatures are all over the place. Some believe that they are nothing more than exotic pets that were discarded when they became too hard to handle. Others pin the creatures as escapees from passing circuses or zoos. Of course, we cannot rule out the possibility of misidentification, hallucinations, and outright hoaxes. But perhaps the answer to this mystery is more paranormal in nature. Researchers theorize that perhaps these creatures have somehow been transported to a different area, time, or even dimension. Even if we end up capturing one of these misplaced creatures, we may never know their true nature.

Hellhounds of Forestville State Park

Where to Encounter It:

Forestville State Park
21071 County Hwy 118
Preston, MN 55965

Directions:

From Wykoff, head south on County Hwy 5 for approximately 6 miles, turn left on County Highway 118 and you will enter the park. There will be signs pointing the way.

Creature Lore:

Throughout history, nearly every culture has told spine-tingling folktales about the demonic hellhounds. These stories were meant to serve as a precautionary warning to younger generations, a precaution that might one day end up saving their lives. To put it mildly, hellhounds are not pretty to look at—in fact, their appearance alone was enough to frighten even the bravest among villagers. The most commonly described appearance of the hellhound is that of a large, heavily-muscled black (sometimes white) dog-like beast with glowing red or green eyes that is also equipped with vicious razor sharp claws and teeth. Occasionally, these beasts would appear to be nearly transparent, allowing the witness to virtually see right through them. Hellhounds caused great trepidation among villagers who tried to avoid them at all costs, because the creatures were thought to roam the night while conducting the Devil's bidding. Those unfortunate souls who were unlucky enough to encounter a hellhound rarely survived to share their experience with others. Those who went missing were often thought to have been victims of the vicious hellhounds, whose intentions could only be imagined in nightmares.

I have spent a good amount of time in Central America, tracking down reports and legends of hellhounds. While in the country of Belize, villagers vehemently warned us not to stay out after dark, because if we did not return by sundown, it would be too dangerous for us to survive—we might encounter one of their hellhounds, called El Cadejos. They warned that if a negro (black) cadejo spotted you, it would supernaturally connect with your spirit and slowly and painfully drain away of all your energy. Unless you could locate a powerful shaman or bush doctor, you would be dead within one week. Even though the majority of cadejo sightings involved the deadly black creature, villagers also told us of several blanco (white) colored beasts as well. Strangely, the white colored creatures were thought to be friendly protectors of humans that would often lead disoriented or drunken wanderers safely back to the village unharmed.

History of Lore:

The former town of Forestville was founded back in 1853 and served as a trading post for rural pioneers and farmers to come and trade goods, swap news, and feel a part of the community. By 1890, with the bypassing of the railroad, the town had all but faded out. Forestville State Park was created in 1963, and now welcomes over 133,000 visitors a year. I wonder just how many of these thousands of vacationers are aware of the park's grisly reputation.

Southern Minnesota has had its share of mysterious creature sightings, which share many similarities with sightings of hellhounds. In 1947 an elusive "cougar" was seen roaming the area south of Winona, Minnesota (1 hour northeast of the state park) before getting spotted farther east in Galesville, Wisconsin, where shocked residents reported seeing the creature lurking around their livestock. One witness told the *Albert Lea Evening Tribune* that even as an experienced hunter "he had never seen an animal of that size running at large." He described it as being "brownish-tan and it was about the size of a Great Dane dog."

In May of 1950, The *Winona Republican Herald* ran a story about the discovery of a bear carcass on a farm in Witoka, Minnesota (45 minutes northeast of the state park). The famer who found the remains "concluded that the animal had been killed by some other animal." Supporting the farmer's theory was the absence of any trapping device located near the bear. With no other possible culprits, the theory was purposed that "the mysterious animal that might have killed the bear could be that big cat or panther which has been reported in the Homer-Witoka and Dakota area."

In October of 1950, another mysterious animal was busy devouring cattle and livestock between the towns of Northrop and Truman, Minnesota (2 hours west of the state park). The *Austin Daily Herald* wrote that eyewitnesses described it as being "five feet long, with a bushy tail and brown stripes." A local farmer discovered the carcass of a freshly-killed calf with its entire hind quarters eaten off. Investigation into the case showed "the animal had been dragged about 25 feet during the night and more of it eaten." A posse of rifleman set out in search of the vicious killer and discovered "clear paw prints four to five inches wide." The prints also showed "four toes and a heel pad and indicated large claws." The mysterious creature was never discovered.

In 1961, another cougar-like creature was once again spotted in Winona County, this time by several Minnesota Sheriff's Deputies. The *Winona Daily News* ran an article on the sighting, quoting Sheriff George Fort: "My deputies saw the cougar four times and had the light on them but the cougar got out of sight when the deputies got out of the car." Not surprising for the times, Sheriff Fort's comments were met with skepticism from the County Board.

Investigation Log:

I included this case with some hesitation, because it appears in only one text and I have not personally received any eyewitness reports that would add to its overall credibility. Each year I receive a couple of dozen reports from people around the world who claim to have come face to face with the deadly hellhounds. Ultimately, even without being contacted by a first-hand eyewitness, I decided that the sheer oddness of the story warranted its inclusion into this guide.

Campsite where the Hellhound attack occurred

The stories of hellhounds terrorizing the park were first reported by Christopher Larsen in his book *Ghosts of Southeastern Minnesota* and recounted in his *Strange Minnesota Monsters* book. In the books, Larsen tells of the terrifying experience of two campers who got a little closer to nature (and death) than they had originally planned. The case began when two friends longing for a fall weekend adventure gathered up a camper and gear and headed off for Forestville State Park. Being that it was the offseason, the park was nearly empty of campers and the pair was placed in secluded site 13 (a supernatural foreshadowing for what was to occur?).

Shortly after arriving, the guys hurriedly set up camp, as night was quickly approaching. Within a few minutes they were busy telling stories around a relaxing, toasty fire. As they sipped on a couple of cold beers, they began to hear something moving around in the darkness. With their senses heightened, they could hear something large snap twigs and shrubs as it stalked the perimeter of their campsite. Whatever was out there must have just been passing through, because the rustling promptly ceased. Turning their attention back to the fire, the friends laughed about how riled up they were getting over nothing. At that very moment something was hurled from the bushes and landed in their fire. Scrambling to get a look, the guys found that a giant dead rat was now being cooked in their roaring fire. Without warning, another dead rat was pitched into the blazing fire. The rats were both quickly scooped out of the fire and placed in a bag inside the camper. At this point the guys believed someone was messing with them, so they gathered up some flashlights and spent the next twenty minutes scouring the darkness in search of the prankster. Finding nothing to explain the weird events, the friends retreated to the safety of the camper to play some cards. Each hand of poker further pushed the odd events out of their mind, when suddenly out of nowhere something crashed into the side of the camper, causing a load thud and rocking the camper. Without hesitation several more thuds hit the camper, accompanied by a horrendous snarling sound coming from right outside the door.

Hellhounds have long been feared throughout the world

From the window, one of the men caught site of two crimson eyes staring back at him from the darkness. Amazingly, he also saw that the creature had a long snout and drooling sharp fangs. The friends were worried that the camper, which was now rocking back and forth and coming up a few feet each time, would tip over on its side. Not knowing the reason why, the friends were convinced that whatever was terrorizing them wanted the rats back. Putting their plan into action, they opened the door in order to toss out the bag containing the two burned rats, but instead of appeasing the beast, the beast shoved its head into the camper entrance and took a slice at one of the guys' wrists. Even more bizarre was their belief that the beast uttered the word "rat" in a raspy growl. In a bizarre twist, one of the guys grabbed a nearby toilet cleaning brush and swatted at the beast. Perhaps the smell or sting of the cleaning chemicals bothered the beast, because it retreated back to the outside darkness. Looking down at his wrist the young man was relieved to find only a grazing cut, and although it was bleeding heavily, it would not be life-threatening. Looking to get out of the park as fast as possible, the men hitched up the camper and dashed into their Jeep to tear out of the park—only to see the ferocious beast standing directly in front of them. The Jeep headlights provided a shocking view of a creature that had to be over eight feet tall. Its body was covered in thick, matted-down fur as it hunched its huge frame in attack position before jumping out of sight. The Jeep raced out of the campsite and the pair made it to the parking lot before realizing the creature was on top of their vehicle. The driver slammed on the brakes, causing the Jeep to come to a sudden stop and causing the beast to tumble forward onto the ground. The driver punched the pedal and heard the thump of the beast as his wheels bounced over its body. The pair of frightened men did not stop driving until they hit the safety of the hospital in Austin, where the injured man received eight stitches, a bloody remembrance to show for his battle with the hellhound. Understandably, the pair vowed never to set foot back into the state park.

Is there enough room inside the park for a hellhound to roam?

Again, I feel the need to reiterate that this case was not personally sent to me and therefore I was unable to speak with either of the witnesses for myself. I don't even have the date or year that the story was said to have happened. The story does seems a bit embellished and weird, but when dealing with the paranormal, what constitutes being "too weird?" If I had failed to investigate every case that I deemed too weird out there, I would have missed out on many weird and credible cases. If we take the case at face value, then the question remains as to what actually attacked them. Is it possible that in all of the adrenaline-filled chaos, the pair mistakenly viewed the attack of a bear as something more supernatural in nature? Certainly the overall size of the beast, the accompaniment of sharp claws, and a body covered in hair/fur would certainly match that of a bear. But what about the other features like the glaring red eyes, the ability to silently leap onto the top of a vehicle, and the raspy vocalization? Do these aspects of the case rule out a bear? Many decades ago it was not all that uncommon for residents of Southern Minnesota to spot a bear or two roaming around, but had there been any recent sightings in the area? I placed a call to Forestville State Park. Looking at all possible explanations for the camper's encounter, I inquired about whether any bear had even been reported near the campground. The warden's answer was emphatic. "No, never, ever." He went on to tell me that in all the years of the state park's existence, not one camper had reported seeing a bear in the vicinity. So if it wasn't a bear, then what was it? Perhaps it was a cougar. Confirmed sightings of cougars in Southern Minnesota are becoming more and more frequent. Yet, outside of the sharp claws and the ability to jump great distances, the rest of the features of the beast do not even come close to fitting that of a cougar. With no other known encounters, we have little else to go on, leaving the possibility of it being a hellhound as a viable option.

Skeptics tend to point out that the park's relatively small 3,170 acres do not provide nearly enough roaming room for a hellhound to go unnoticed. This would turn out to be a valid point if, indeed, hellhounds are flesh and blood creatures. More and more researchers, myself included, hold open the possibility that hellhounds may not be a natural earth animal like a bear or cougar. Instead, hellhounds exhibit characteristics of being not of this earth—like super speed, strength, and the ability to appear and disappear at will—leading some to speculate that they are from another place, dimension, or even time. Others contend that hellhounds are a Tulpa or thought-form creature, meaning that over the many years of human belief, story-telling and fears have caused the imaginary beast to manifest into an actual creature. If any of these theories regarding the hellhounds are accurate, it would make the argument over the amount of space available for them to roam truly irrelevant.

In the summer of 2011, I traveled to Forestville State Park in search of hellhounds with veteran legend trippers Noah Voss, Kevin Nelson, Todd Roll, and Jesse Donahue. Although the park was full of visiting campers, several of the sites—including the alleged hot spot of number 13—were still open, allowing us to scour the area in search of any evidence of hellhound activity. Unfortunately, our investigation turned up little in terms of encountering a hellhound or discovering evidence of its existence or whereabouts. I like to think that just maybe the hellhound is still patrolling the state park, waiting for its next victims to pull in.

The Wendigo of Ross

Where To Encounter It:

Rural Roads
Ross, MN

Directions:

The Wendigo creature has most frequently been sighted along the back roads of the area.

Creature Lore:

Alternate spellings: We-Te Go, Windigo, Witigo, Wiindigoo, Windago and many others.

Born from Native American legends, the tale of the Wendigo is both cautionary and horrifying. The most widely held belief tells of unfortunate souls who become lost in the deep forests of the Northwoods. With little food and water, the trapped individual resorts to cannibalism in order to survive, an act so barbaric that it transforms them into the cursed Wendigo. Other legends tell of Native American medicine men or shamans who stray from their healing path and pursue the dark side of black magic. Their punishment for such indiscretion is to be cursed to eternally walk the earth in the form of a hideous cannibal known as the Wendigo.

Traditional descriptions of the Wendigo tell of a dreadful looking creature that is extremely tall and lanky and whose body is twisted and withered in muscle-deprived bone. Its discolored skin is covered in filthy spotted patches of hair covered with the remnants of its unspeakable acts. Often sightings of the Wendigo are placed alongside sightings of Bigfoot or Sasquatch creatures, even though the Wendigo appears to be a totally unrelated creature. In fact, in his book, *Big Footprints*, anthropologist Grover Krantz discounts the idea that the Wendigo is merely another name for those who encounter a Sasquatch, writing, "Wendigo mostly describe natives who have turned into cannibals; it is only with some difficulty that a Sasquatch image can be read into this."

History of Lore:

One of the most troubling accounts of a Wendigo comes from the sensational story of a Native American Chief named Jack Fiddler who was responsible for killing over 25 members of his Canadian tribe. Fiddler claimed that all of his kills were done to rid the victims of the evil Wendigo spirit that possessed their bodies and souls. One case involved a young Indian woman who suddenly became ill and began acting delirious. In order to ensure that her spirit made it to the great hunting grounds, Chief Fiddler preformed a cleansing ritual before ending the woman's suffering by strangling her to death. On October 20, 1907, the *Washington Post* printed the chief's belief that the killing actually freed the woman, because "if she lived she would be a crazy cannibal, devouring her own children and the devil, or We-te-go, would go into other members of the tribe." Eventually Fiddler was caught but committed suicide before he could be tried for his crimes.

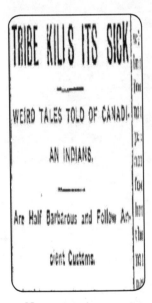

Newspaper account of the horrific tribal killings

During the late 1800s, the Township of Ross, Minnesota was known as Indian Village and was mainly inhabited by forty or fifty Native Americans, along with a handful of pioneer families. One of the early white settlers, Jake Nelson, kept detailed journals of his time in Indian Village, which were published as the manuscript *Forty Years in the Roseau Valley*. Most of the journal is filled with standard history topics, first settlers, tragic fires, hunting and fishing expeditions, and the like. Yet, hidden among the more mundane happenings of the area are two intriguing entries where Nelson details the area's paranormal legends.

Investigation Log:

In 1886, Nelson was working on the construction of his family's home when he "noticed a light by a bunch of willows near the muskeg," about a quarter of a mile from Indian Village. Intrigued by the floating light, Nelson asked his friend Billy McGillis if any of the Indians were out camping in the area, thinking their campfires might be the cause of the light. McGillis explained that the light was actually caused by some type of gas rising out of the nearby muskeg. According to legend, the light would show up in the exact spot each and every year while the Indians unsuccessfully attempted to catch it. Even Nelson tried his hand at capturing the light, writing, "It seemed to float around us and then return to the same place." Over the years, others also sought to wrangle up the light, but each gave up claiming that it was too much like "playing tag with the Devil." The mystery of the light has never been fully explained. Skeptics tend to agree with the explanation put forth by McGillis that these lights are nothing more than swamp gas that produces the baffling light show. On the flipside, many contend that these mysterious lights function as though they are controlled by some intelligent force, possibly even by spirits of the dead.

Nelson also wrote quite a bit about the life and culture of the native people living at Indian Village, even detailing some of their superstitions and paranormal beliefs. One such legend told of a creature so bizarre that it stood out to Nelson, who called it the "Ghost of the Indian River." The natives called it the "Windago" and had encountered the creature many times before and believed that the beast was a harbinger of death, as it always seemed to presage the death of someone living in the village. Nelson explained that the creature had been known to the Indians for so long "that they have no traditions of its first appearance." According to

Nelson, the first white people to encounter the apparition were Edina Nelson and her brother, Jesse. The siblings were walking to school about a mile west of the village when "they met the apparition in the road." They described the creature as being "eight feet tall dressed in white and having on its forehead, a large bright star." Nelson claimed that shortly after the odd sighting, death once again paid a visit to the village.

Even stranger yet is the story Nelson tells of one Mrs. Mickinock, who had been ill for several days. She was being cared for by her granddaughter, Anna Mickinock. Anna was in the yard of her grandmother along with Nelson's mother, his sister and Mrs. Warner when Anna stated, "Grandma die pretty soon." She pointed to a "very tall person, dressed in white" walking across the prairie that disappeared from sight near a grove on a small ridge. Sure enough, consistent with the legend, the very next day death took Grandma Mickinock. Her death should not have come as a surprise, because in an even more bizarre twist to the story, the villagers claimed that Mickinock was over 150 years old. Nelson told of many very old Indians who lived in the village and none of them "knew anything about the childhood days of the old lady."

Although Nelson wrote highly of the natives, he had to believe that the creature was nothing more than Native American superstition—that is, until he spotted the spirit with his own eyes. It came when the young Mickinock family headed off to Canada on a hunting expedition. During the hunt the wife became ill, sat down, and exclaimed that death had taken control of her. Packing up, the family quickly departed Canada and headed back to Indian Village. Three days after their return, Nelson was in their yard during the afternoon when he saw that "the apparition had risen by the side of the muskeg." Nelson watched the spirit stumble and nearly fall as it passed out of his line of sight. Nelson described the creature as being about "fifteen feet tall, dressed in white lace or some similar material," carrying some type of package in its right hand. By the following morning, the wife was dead.

Rural road where the Wendigo has frequently appeared

After seeing the "Windago" with his own eyes, Nelson speculated on the true identity of the spirit, writing, "It is generally supposed that ghosts walk only at night, but all of the appearances of the above mentioned were in broad daylight and in bright sunshine, whatever it may have been, it was not a hallucination of superstitious fears in the dark."

The Township of Ross is located deep in the Northwoods of Minnesota near the Canadian border, which is fitting due to the abundance of Wendigo sightings that have occurred in Canada. Having been on two separate expeditions in search of the Canadian Wendigo, each of which provided a smattering of first-hand stories, I was excited to once again pursue the creature. In 2004, with a

105

long drive ahead of me, I set off for Ross hoping to get closer to the truth of what type of being was roaming the countryside. As the hours passed, I struggled to put an overall picture of this creature together…too many pieces still remained unknown. While Nelson's journal is indispensible to this case, it offers no definitive answers and at times is even confusing with the varying descriptions of the spirit/apparition/ghost/wendago. On one occasion the thing is reported to be over 8 feet tall, yet when it is spotted again it is thought to be 15 feet tall. The only consistent aspect of the beast was that it always seemed to be adorned in white. The white lace or material worn by the beast is an interesting feature and bears resemblance to the traditional sightings of a white skinned/furred Wendigo. The bright glowing star-shaped object that decorated the forehead of the creature also seems to be an outlier, driving it closer to the general appearance of a spirit or apparition rather than a flesh and blood animal. From the journals alone it is hard to distinguish the physical makeup of the being. I decided that the only way to discover the truth behind the legend was to explore the land of Indian Village (Ross). With any luck, my digging around the township might just reveal some additional legends of the Wendigo.

Pulling in to tiny township of 450 residents, I half expected them to chuckle as they flippantly declared that the Wendigo is nothing more than a Native American superstition from a time long since passed. On the contrary, I found that not only did the locals not scoff at the idea, they were actually willing to share some of the most recent sightings. I spoke with a couple of local historians who, over the last twenty years, have kept unofficial records of upwards of ten different witnesses that encountered the Wendigo while traveling the back roads of Ross. Unlike the sightings of the past, all of which shared several similarities, each of the more recent accounts differed greatly from one sighting to the next. In the modern sightings, the appearance of the creature spanned the entire spectrum…from those who believed that it was a flesh and blood living creature, to those who claimed that they could see right through the being and believed it to be more of a supernatural or spiritual entity. The gender of the creature was another sticking point; the Wendigo appeared in the form of a female to some, while others swore that it was a male. And, unlike all of the previous encounters, which were exclusively day time sightings, several of the recent cases occurred during the wee hours of the night. Based on all the reports, the one commonality was that the Wendigo was thought to be a biped, as all of the witnesses spotted it standing and walking on its hind legs as do humans.

Interestingly, the historians mentioned that a couple of the witnesses talked about a bright light that accompanied the creature. For me the inclusion of the light detail adds to the credibility of the sightings, as the only place that this is mentioned is in the obscure journal of Jake Nelson, which is not a best-selling manuscript. Of course, the mentioning of the light could be simply coincidental or tailored on Bigfoot accounts where mysterious lights have appeared in the vicinity of the creature.

In studying the paranormal/folklore, I am always fascinated by the morphing and/or progression that a legend goes through. As the years roll by, often times the legend will transform itself into something else. Sometimes the change is subtle like a changing of the date or name, while other legends are altered so drastically they take on a complete life of their own. In this case, the harbinger of death aspect has all but been dropped from the legend. The historians assured me that, although multiple recent sightings have been reported, they were not aware of any known deaths attributed to the sightings.

During my investigation of the Wendigo, I spent several days scouring the back roads of Ross in search of the creature. I set up motion detectors, night vision cameras, trail cams, and staked out the area with the optimistic expectation of coming face to face with the Wendigo. Once again, I was forced to leave the area with little more evidence than re-told stories of encounters of the beast. During my trip home, the case of the Ross Wendigo remained as mysterious and unexplained to me as it did to Jake Nelson.

Bertha - The Witch of Trout Lake Cemetery

Where To Encounter It:

Trout Lake-Lakeside Cemetery
Crooked Road
Coleraine, MN

Directions:

From Highway 169, turn onto 10 West. From 10 West, turn onto Crooked Road. The cemetery will be on the right hand side.

The cemetery has been victim to countless attacks of vandalism. Please enter the area with respect and abide by all posted hours and rules.

Creature Lore:

Thanks to Hollywood's recent erroneous interpretation of witches through shows like *Sabrina the Teenage Witch, Charmed,* and *Harry Potter,* people's perception of them is at odds with the more historically traditional view. In days of old, being a witch was not the wisest of career choices. Faced with a life of being feared, misunderstood, ostracized, imprisoned, or even sentenced to a brutal death wasn't too appealing. Witches historically have been viewed as social outcasts, practicing the dark art of witchcraft while closely aligning themselves with demonic forces and even the Devil himself. But are witches actual creatures? Or are they simply those who chose to practice Wicca long before it was socially accepted? This question has sparked deep debate among researchers who question the actual physical makeup of a witch. Are they normal, rational men and women whose earth-based rituals and spells are simply misunderstood? Or are they some type of unknown cryptozoological creature?

Even the extent of the strength and power of these witchcraft practitioners varies widely throughout folklore. Thought to possess deadly supernatural powers, witches were able to inflect great physical, mental, and spiritual harm to those who fell under their wrath. The work of witches and witchcraft was routinely blamed for poor harvests, sudden illnesses, loss of livestock, and even the disappearance of small children. Even today, the popular perception of a "traditional" witch is that of a hideous old woman whose pitch black clothing is matched only by her cold heart. Yet, this wasn't always the case; one of the many powers of witches is thought to be their ability to shape shift and transform themselves into many different forms. They often would operate under guise of animals or morph into young attractive girls in order to achieve their unholy objectives.

History of Lore:

If you look online, you find some confusion over the proper name of the cemetery, as it is listed as Lakeside, Trout Lake, and the Norwegian Cemetery. Currently, the official name is listed as the Trout Lake-Lakeside Cemetery.

The woman thought to be the witch haunting the cemetery is that of Bertha Maynard, who was born January 26th, 1872 and died on January 27th, 1910. Upon her death, Bertha was one of the first people to be buried inside the cemetery. One of her teenage sons did the honor of digging his mother's grave as her grieving family watched nearby. Over the years, Bertha's gravestone has been plagued with trouble. Thieves or pranksters steal or move the pillar, only to have it recovered by local police or maintenance workers. They would then return it to its proper place, only to have the cycle repeat itself. Finally, after years of continual mischief, the cemetery decided that in order to ensure the safety of the marker, they would house it in their maintenance building. This is probably where the legend of the missing stone originated…even though the stone wasn't missing, it was just removed. Eventually, Bertha's family grew tired of having no stone to pay their respects at and requested that the stone be replaced at its proper site. The pillar was safely brought back to the gravesite and remained there for several years until the cycle began anew—the pillar was once again taken and has been missing since 2009. To combat visitors driving into the cemetery, the caretakers have erected a front fence to help slow down the incidents of vandalism.

In the 1960s, the Norwegian Church that had sat next to the cemetery was removed, and the cemetery was all but abandoned. I spoke with the current caretakers of the cemetery who informed me that after the removal of the church, the cemetery became a favorite party spot for local teenagers. According to the caretakers, the removal of the church corresponded with the initial legends about Bertha. However, the now defunct Northern Minnesota Paranormal Investigators (NMPI) believed that they had traced the legend of Bertha back to the early 1920s.

Investigation Log:

There are many legends surrounding the death and burial of Bertha Maynard. One of the more popular (and sinister) versions tells of a young woman practicing witchcraft within the community back in the early 1900s. Fearing that her dabbling in black magic would attract evil spirits to the town, the residents took matters into their own hands and sent the young witch to her grave. Following the customs of the time, the local townsfolk dared not bury the witch inside the cemetery proper, so they were forced to bury her down at the bottom of a hill just outside of the consecrated grounds. Angered by the unpunished act of her murder and the manner in which she received an improper burial, the witch is forever condemned to spend eternity at her gravesite, where she waits patiently for unsuspecting visitors to wander over her way where she can exact her revenge.

Bertha's gravestone

The main legend told above has spawned all sorts of paranormal reports within the cemetery. The gravestone itself has been the center of many tales (most likely due to its repeated disappearance and reappearance). It is said that those who are brave (or foolish) enough to visit the gravesite will see the gravestone move and dart around the cemetery. Even more disturbing are the reports from those who actually see the grave pillar disappear right before their eyes. One of the more fascinating legends of the tombstone is the dare that no matter how many times you try, or how many different cameras you use, you will not be able to successfully take a picture of the witch's grave.

Other more terrifying reports at the cemetery have surfaced as well. One such legend states that when visitors reach Bertha's site, they become overwhelmed by an uneasy feeling washing over them, as though they are not wanted inside the cemetery and should leave immediately lest something bad befalls upon them.

It goes without saying that the cemetery is a hotbed for legend trippers, and one of their favorite activities while exploring the cemetery is to walk around with an audio recorder looking to capture any ghostly voices or sounds (EVPs) that are not audible to the human ear. On many occasions, visitors have captured the sound of a female voice that is believed to be from Bertha the Witch. In addition to the ghostly voices caught on audio, many visitors report seeing the apparition of a female spirit roaming the cemetery. Although many believe the spirit is that of Bertha, the identity of the apparition is unknown.

The anomalies of the cemetery are not limited to audio recorders, as evidenced by the numerous photos taken within the cemetery that often capture strange balls of light (orbs) or mysterious forms of mist or smoke-like substances that many believe show the spirit of the witch.

It appears that many of the abovementioned legends have sprouted out due to the location of Bertha's grave. In fact, her grave is located in a secluded area at the bottom of a hill, an area that is devoid of other gravesites. Rather than having a paranormal explanation, the location of her grave was based more on Bertha occupying one of the original burial spots inside the cemetery. Most likely, future families took into consideration the frequent flooding of the lower area and decided to move the burials onto dryer ground, thus leaving Bertha all alone in her damp resting spot.

A mysterious fog-like substance appears in a photo taken by Brian Leffler.

The matter of whether or not Bertha was actually a witch has become a contentious subject among investigators. With no way to definitively prove or disprove this claim, the idea that she was a witch seems to win out by default. If Bertha was indeed a witch, she seemed to break away from the stereotypical behavior we normally associate with witches, like living alone in a secluded country home (Bertha had a husband and several children), being despised by her peers (Bertha's husband, Charles, held an important and respected job in local government), and dying in a peculiar manner. The last one (her death) is one of the more puzzling aspects of this case. I spoke with the Itasca County Recorder, which handles all of the birth, death, and marriage licenses for the county and discovered that they had no death record for either Bertha or Charles Maynard. This normally could be easily explained away by the fact that the deceased simply died while living or visiting another county. However, the records department was unable to locate any death certificate for Bertha in the entire state of Minnesota. Neither the cemetery caretakers nor the Itasca County Historical Society knew of a cause of death. Perhaps Bertha passed away in another state or her death certificate was simply lost in a fire or similar tragedy, but regardless of the circumstances, I am forced to leave her cause of death unknown.

Another strange photo snapped by Brian Leffler.

Over the years I have teeter totted on this case, struggling to decide what to make of it. On the one hand, I have visited this cemetery on several different occasions and each time Bertha's pillar was visible, it remained stationary and showed up in all of my photos, and I was lucky enough to have been spared from Bertha's wrath. Yet, at the same time, there is much to push me towards believing—from the countless credible firsthand witness accounts, to the unexplained photos that purport to show Bertha haunting the cemetery. I guess that until I gather enough evidence on either side to come to an absolute conclusion, I will have to consider this case an unsolved mystery, which makes it all the more exciting.

The Witches of Loon Lake Cemetery

Where to Encounter It:

Mary's Gravestone –
Jackson County Historical
Society
307 N Highway 86
Lakefield, MN 56150-1259
(507) 662-5505

Loon Lake Cemetery –
48804 Highway 4
Jackson, MN 56143
1-888-293-4446

Directions:

Jackson County Historical Society – The historical society/museum is located in the heart of downtown Lakefield, Minnesota. The main road runs through town, and you will have no problem finding it.

Loon Lake Cemetery – From Lakefield travel south on Highway 86 until you reach County Road 4 (720th St.), Turn left and head east. Stay on 4 until you see signs for Robertson Park on your left and pull into the main gate. When you enter the park you will pass through the green gate and proceed to the fork in the road, where you want to stay right. There you will find a small parking area where you need to get out and walk along the trail for ¼ mile to the cemetery.

Creature Lore:

One of the more interesting aspects regarding the legend of witches is the manner in which they are intertwined with curses and cursed objects. Reasons for witches placing curses are as bountiful as stories of witches themselves. Common accounts of curses turn up tales of jealously, love, envy, and retribution for being spurned by their communities. The purpose of placing a curse on someone would often center around causing poor health, misfortune, terrible luck, economic disaster, and such as this case, even death. Over the years, witches were gradually placed in the same category as werewolves, vampires, demons, and other denizens of the Devil. They became fearful objects of overly superstitious settlers who carried their beliefs and folklore with them to this new country. Witches were routinely blamed for crops that failed to produce, people dying from unknown illnesses, children going missing, and sickly livestock. Terrified residents took numerous precautions to protect themselves from witches. Everything from carrying holy water, salt, amulets, and horseshoes, were adhered to in order to protect oneself from witches—all of which may serve you well while investigating this case.

History of Lore:

In my travels around the globe, I have become no stranger to the folklore surrounding witches and their curses. In Wisconsin, Witch (Callen) Road is plagued by sightings of an evil witch hell-bent on taking revenge on those foolish enough to venture out there. In Iowa, those who visit Oak Hill Cemetery in Cedar Rapids find themselves haunted by Tillie—an alleged witch who was stoned to death—who now resides inside the cemetery. In Illinois, the small town of Chesterville has its own witch that rests in a grave directly under a giant tree in the town cemetery. Legend states that if you are brave enough to touch the tree at exactly midnight, the vengeful witch will make herself known. Of course, in other countries, the belief in witches is more prevalent than here in the U.S. During my multiple expeditions into Central America, I was repeatedly warned to stay away from witches, and no matter what creature I was out searching for, people reminded me to heed their advice and protect myself from the evil magic of witches.

Investigation Log:

There are so many versions of the Loon Lake Cemetery legend that the actual truth has all but been forgotten by those simply looking to scare themselves with a creepy tale of witchcraft, murder, and revenge. To help simplify the legends, I will try to sort the facts from fiction.

The overgrown path that leads to the secluded cemetery

The most well-known and ominous of the legend tells of a young woman named Mary Jane Twiliger (Twillegar, Twiliger, Terwilleger, etc…), who was involved in the practice of witchcraft. Being that it was the 1800s, the overly superstitious among the community did not look kindly on Mary's Devilish rituals and set out to put an end to it—which they did by chopping off Mary's head with an axe. Mary's gruesome body, along with the bloody axe, was buried in Loon Lake cemetery. With her burial, the townsfolk believed that it was the end of the story. However, as they would soon find out, the story was just beginning. Shortly after Mary's death, residents began to whisper about strange happenings out at the cemetery, which were immediately attributed to Mary's vengeful spirit. A few short years later, Clarinda Allen, another suspected young witch, was also decapitated and buried out at the cemetery. The town must have been plagued with witches, because legend tells of a third young woman who met her fate at the hands of the frightened and murderous community. Unfortunately, the third woman's name has been lost to history. The Loon Lake Cemetery was quickly filling up with suspected witches, which gave rise to the stories of the place being cursed. Over the years, the legends grew to monstrous proportions…eventually leading to the tale that anyone who is foolish enough to jump over the graves of the murdered witches would suffer tremendous bouts of bad luck and may even die due to their unwise decisions.

The wild and overgrown cemetery

It is an amazing legend, but is any of it actually true? The answer to that question is a bit trickier that a simple yes or no. First of all, it looks as though 17-year-old Mary Terwilliger was not beheaded at all. According to the March 18, 1880 edition of the *Spirit Lake Beacon*, Mary met death at the hands of the more mundane manner of diphtheria while living in Cherokee County, Iowa. Mary's body was originally buried in Spirit Lake until her family moved to Minnesota and decided to reinter Mary's body at the Loon Lake Cemetery. As for the other two alleged witches, no known evidence has been found to either dismiss or substantiate the claims.

Due to the overwhelming amount of vandalism that has occurred at the cemetery, Mary's gravestone was removed from the cemetery and placed in the safety of the Jackson County Historical Society, where it remains on display to the public. I stopped in to speak with several of the historical society's researchers, who believed that the legend of Mary was created by a local man named James Peters. He was, by all accounts, an eccentric fellow who was widely known to have believed in witches. There is also some speculation that perhaps Peters promoted or even concocted the story in order to keep away trespassers from his land—a misguided idea that never actually worked out. A more plausible theory is that Peters, who had created an effigy of a witch on his land to protect himself, was truly convinced that witches had inhabited the cemetery and he looked to spread the word. There are others who claim that contrary to Peters' original intent, the story was made up to attract more tourists and money to the area. If this is the case, the plan has certainly worked. The museum researchers also guided me to the display of Mary's gravestone. Expressing concern, they told me that the gravestone had been removed to protect it from vandals. In fact, the cemetery is due for a complete overhaul, as the museum does have burial records for some of the people resting there and are eager to repair the damaged stones and clean up the overgrowth as funds allow. After many years of getting requests for information about Mary, the society is working on a book that would set the record straight on the detailed history of the cemetery.

Unfortunately many of the remaining graves have been vandalized

After visiting with the museum staff, I headed out to the cemetery itself. Now I point out that at Loon Lake Cemetery, the belief and fearfulness expressed in witches rivals that of anything I have encountered in my international travels. Without a doubt, the story of Loon Lake Cemetery is one of Minnesota's most well-known and most feared legends. If there is any cemetery in Minnesota that looks like it should be haunted, Loon Lake is it. It has all the Hollywood trademarks of a haunted cemetery, with the eeriness of the area beginning right as you make your way through the small county-run park and begin to notice the seclusion of the area starting to creep in. If anything goes wrong, you best be prepared…because help would not arrive for quite some time. As you meander along the overgrown trail that leads up to the cemetery, the mixture of the isolation and the apparent lack of any cemetery caretaking all but dares you to discover the graves of the witches. If you make it out to the overgrown cemetery, you have completed the easy portion of the adventure. Now the hard work begins. You must struggle to locate the location of the witches' graves—a nearly impossible task given that no one is truly certain where the graves in question are located. As you will

soon discover, the graveyard is in complete disarray, nearly all of the stones have been vandalized, broken, or kicked over. Compile that with the lush overgrowth of the sounding grasses, shrubs, and trees, and the place becomes nearly unnavigable. Yet even with its difficult terrain, Loon Lake Cemetery produces more paranormal encounters than you can imagine.

Mary's gravestone

After one of my presentations, a young woman approached me and asked if I knew of any way to break the Look Lake curse. Apparently, she had gone out the cemetery late at night with a group of friends. One of her brother's friends, looking to show off his bravery to the captive audience, decided to jump over as many gravesites as he could while mocking the legend the entire time. As the night progressed, the group began to get bored since nothing out of the ordinary was happening and returned home disappointed. The next day, the young woman was awoken by her phone ringing. On the other end was her brother. He informed her that after dropping everybody off, the daring grave-jumping young man was involved in a serious car accident that placed him in the hospital. Luckily the young man survived the accident, and although she told me that she would have him call me to confirm, I never heard a follow-up about the case. Perhaps my curse-breaking advice did the trick, and the man is still out there happily tempting fate whenever he can.

I frequently encounter people who have ventured out to the cemetery in order to check out the legend. The overwhelming majority of these legend trippers wisely elect to pass up the opportunity to bring bad luck upon themselves, yet this does not affect their chances of experiencing something paranormal. I have received several reports from legend trippers who, while out at the cemetery, get overwhelmed with the feeling that something "else" is there with them. On several occasions, witnesses have even spotted the apparition of a young woman floating through the area—whether she is the spirit of Mary Jane remains unknown. Others tell of seeing mysterious flying lights, unknown sounds, and the general uneasy feeling that seems to be the graveyard's trademark.

One of the more interesting and creepy aspects of the cemetery is the ability of visitors to spend the night in the nearby park campground.

For those who have done so, they often report hearing the faint wailing of a female voice drifting out from the area of the cemetery. One such camper contacted me after spending a nearly sleepless night sitting up inside his tent while trying to figure out where the womanly cries were coming from. Believing that a relaxing camping trip was actually what he needed to de-stress from a hectic work week, the young man departed for the campground. While setting up his tent, he marveled at the peacefulness of the area. Little did he know that the atmosphere was about to take a turn for the worse. Tucked inside his two-person tent, the young man eased back and enjoyed the quietness as he prepared for a good night's sleep. Trying to keep his mind from thoughts of work, the quiet was broken by the sound of a woman talking in a voice so slight that he was unable to make out what she was saying. Unzipping his tent, he stuck out his head hoping to see a fellow camper passing by. Only the stars in the sky were outside as the man popped back into the tent and quickly settled in. Just before dozing off, the voice returned…this time it was a bit louder, but it still remained unintelligible. Convinced that someone was trying to scare him or playing a trick, he grabbed his flashlight and headed out to investigate. Again, the frustrated man found the area completely empty. Now a pattern was starting to emerge whereby every time he was closing in on sleep, the female voice would interrupt, forcing him to sit up and listen. This bizarre ritual was repeated several more times, and each time the man would sit up and listen intently for the source of the voice, which never came. Finally morning arrived and the drowsy young man packed up and prepared to leave. On his way out he stopped into the office to ask if anyone else had reported anything similar that evening. The man stated that the voice sounded as though it was coming from the area by the hill, only to discover that the area of the voice was exactly where the cemetery was. Not one to believe in ghost stories, after hearing the legends of the place the man hoped that the voice was that of a late-night cemetery visitor, but still he told me that he wasn't in any hurry to return.

The internet is overrun with paranormal stories from those who visit the cemetery. Everything from accidents and work firings to speeding tickets and death have been blamed on the cemetery. There remains no documented case of anyone passing away after visiting the grave of Mary Jane. But then again, if these people did die due to their cemetery visit, they wouldn't be in a position to tell anyone.

The Little People of the Pipestone National Monument

Where to Encounter It:

Pipestone National Monument
36 Reservation Avenue
Pipestone, MN 56164
(507) 825-5464

Directions:

From downtown Pipestone, take Hiawatha Ave. to the north. Turn right on Reservation Ave. and follow it to the monument. (There are numerous road signs that will guide you there.)

Creature Lore:

Folklore is filled with accounts of gnomes, fairies, little people, wee folk, and the like. Regardless of the title bestowed on them, their locations, or even the time period in which they are reported, these creatures share many characteristics. First, many cultures also believe these creatures are shape-shifters, giving them the ability to morph into nearly any type of animal or person making their detection extremely challenging. Even more frightening, they are almost always regarded as supernatural beings that posses the power to curse you with bad luck or to steal your eyesight, hearing, or even your life. When dealing with the little people, it was thought wise to avoid any contact, lest you be drawn under their magical spell. However, these creatures also exhibit a playful side, enjoying frequent rues, tricks, games, and other behavior that would be classified more as joking than deadly. Those who hold a more sinister outlook on the deviously clever creatures tell of them luring children away from the parents where they are kept for some unknown nefarious purpose. In order to cover their tracks, the creatures simply replace the abducted children with identical looking beings known as changelings.

When I was in the county of Belize, I was roaming their vast forests in search of a jungle protector called the Tata Duende, who is said to prey on anyone caught disrespecting the land. The Duende was said to lure those offenders off to a hidden lair where their dismembered remains would never see the light of day. While there, I talked with a forest ranger who as a child had a bizarre run in with the Duende. He told me that while playing in a nearby wooded area, he spotted the diminutive Duende standing off in the distance. The creature was motioning with his arms as though to beckon the young boy toward him. At the same time, the boy heard a beautiful song being sung by the Duende that seemed to put the young boy under some type of trance or spell. He remembered mindlessly walking toward the creature, when suddenly the spell was shattered by the voice of his mother calling out for him to return home. After re-telling his story, the ranger asked me why in the heck I would ever actively search for the Duende.

Having spent years studying the folklore behind the little people, it wasn't until my expedition to Ireland that I began a serious effort to protect myself while searching for gnomes and fairies. While researching the Emerald Isle, I encountered many local residents who imparted this advice: when dealing with the little folk, one should always bring along an offering to ward off their supernatural powers. These offerings could be anything from a bright shiny rock to that of some skittles or other form of candy. The Native Americans of the US recommend leaving tobacco as an attempt to insulate oneself from the powers of the little people. I had no idea at the time that this advice was mere foreshadowing for my adventure into the little people of Pipestone National Monument.

History of Lore:

The area of Pipestone National Monument is considered sacred by the Native people. According to Sioux legend, the Great Spirit arrived in the form of a giant bird and summoned together all of the surrounding tribes to him. With all of his people gathered before him, he broke out a piece of the red stone and molded it into a pipe and smoked it. The Great Spirit spoke to the tribes, telling them that the red stone was their flesh and that all smoke to him must come from nothing but the red stone. Native folklore also tells the tragic story of the creation of the stone's wonderful red tone. Many years ago the water of the river began to flood, causing widespread drowning among the tribe that dwelled near its banks.

Eventually, the toll of the flood took the lives of all but one and only a sole fair maiden remained on an isolated patch of non-flooded land. Surrounded by water, the woman was visited by a spirit that descended upon the patch of land telling the maiden that he wished to make her his wife and start a new population. The blood from the countless flood victims rushed through the river and turned all of the stone to red, thus adding to the legend that the stone is actually the flesh and blood of the people.

For hundreds of years, Native Americans have been returning to Pipestone to quarry the red stone and continue to hold the land in the highest regard as a sacred site. According to legend, the place has always exhibited a peaceful presence; no matter what wars, rivalries, or skirmishes the various tribes were involved in, they put these differences aside and declared peace while at Pipestone. It was also with the first natives that the stories of the little people began to be whispered through the generations. In an effort to diminish the ill effects of the little people, these stories contained the barest of details, only warning each subsequent generation that the little people were present and that they should be left alone.

Investigation Log:

I first learned of the legend of the Pipestone little people while I was in town giving a lecture on the haunted locations of Minnesota. After the lecture, a woman recalled her bizarre experience while out at the national monument. It was just before dusk, and the woman was out hiking with a couple of friends when she made out the faint sounds of a singing female voice. Puzzled by the fact that her companions were unable to hear the beautiful singing, the group remained motionless as they listened for the wails. After a few moments of intense listening, the second friend began to hear the faint singing, yet for the third woman the singing remained inaudible. Knowing that a lot of ceremonies are held at the monument, the women attempted to follow the voice in order to discovery its origin, yet every time they followed the sound, it seemed to move around them as though they were unknowingly engaged in a game of hide and seek. Finally, the frustrated group gave up on their endeavor and exited the monument unsure of what had just transpired.

A nearly perfect location for little people to inhabit

The hiking women may not be alone in their experience with something weird out at the monument. In their book, *Pipestone Ghost Stories 2,* the Pipestone County Historical Society details the accounts of those who report that the little people have the ability to change shapes and can appear in the form of various animals or people. One such account tells of a father and his son walking their dog along the monument trail. Just like the previous story, it was dusk when they "heard a chorus of Native American women singing in the trees." Even though they were pretty certain of the location of the singing, the two men discovered that no one was there—at least not anyone they could see.

Another case also comes from the book *Pipestone Ghost Stories 2,* where a local Pipestone resident decided to participate in the Sundance, a religious event that is held annually at the monument. While camping overnight in a teepee, her peaceful sleep was broken by the sound of children playing outside. Curious, the woman peeked her head out of the door where only darkness greeted her. Thinking it must have been a dream, she laid back down to sleep only to hear the children playing once again. She wondered what the children were doing out at such a late hour, and just as she was about to go out and scold the children a set of foot-sized indentations vertically ran up the side of her teepee. Bravely, the woman once again peered out the opening—only to find the area completely devoid of children. Needless to say, the woman slept little after her encounter with the little people.

The quarry is considered a sacred site

Inquiring around town, I was surprised to discover that nearly all of the residents I spoke with were familiar with the tales of the little people inhabiting the monument. My colleague, Terry Fisk, had investigated the monument years before and collected several odd cases from some of the employees. Terry spoke with a former maintenance worker who would often hear mysterious sounds while cleaning up the "empty" visitor's center. Others that Terry spoke with expressed the opinion that without a doubt the little people were real. My years of research have taught me that best way to ascertain the validity of legends is to try and experience them for yourself. With this in mind, I ventured out to the monument and struck up a conversation with one of the pipe carvers. He told me that the carvers keep many of their pipes and pieces of stone artwork back in a storage room, and on many occasions carvers have heard the sound of the pipes rattling or being lightly tapped together as though someone or something was playing with them. Each time the workers would go to check out the sound, they would find the room completely empty and the rattling would abruptly cease.

It seems that the little people are not exclusively confined to the monument, as evidenced by this next case that comes from the book *Pipestone Ghost Stories*. The story goes like this: one evening a young boy was excited to see the arrival of his uncle who led him out into the corn field to play. Once in the field, the boy lost sight of his uncle, wandered back home and explained the bizarre situation to his worried parents. The only problem with his story was the fact the uncle had died years before his late-night visit to his nephew. The family believed that the whole incident could be attributed to the mischievous work of the little people.

During my second expedition to the monument, I was staying in downtown Pipestone at the Calumet Hotel, which has a long history of haunted activity. Having survived the town's evening ghost walk and my stay in the haunted room, I decided to take advantage of the beautifully sunny afternoon and walk the short 1.5 miles out to the monument. There was not a cloud in the sky as I leisurely strolled along, enjoying the scenic beauty of the area. Upon arriving at the monument, I headed directly to a secluded location that I felt would be perfect for spotting a little person. I was armed with an offering in the form of a handful of M&Ms that I neatly placed in a small pile in hopes of enticing the little people to show themselves—or at the very least to protect me from their supernatural powers. As I patiently sat on a nearby bench under a lovely shade tree, I felt something "land" in my hair. Thinking it was nothing more than falling debris from the one of the hanging tree branches, I ran my hand through my hair only to discover that nothing was there. Passing it off, I began to concentrate on seeing the little people, even vocally calling out for them to make themselves known. As the minutes ticked by, I slowly began to feel a bit drowsy, which was odd because it was still early afternoon and my body was revved up from the hike to the monument. Looking over to my right, I noticed that my M&M offering was still sitting there untouched; meanwhile I was drifting deeper and deeper into drowsiness. Finally, in an effort to stave off sleep, I tiredly stood up and walked back to the visitor's center, hoping that it would help me garner up some lost energy.

The small offering I left for the little people to avoid being cursed

Never in all my years of research had drowsiness set in so quickly, but surprisingly the very minute I entered the building I began to rebound from my bout of lethargy. The rebounding of energy was startling, but as I tried to rationalize it I thought that maybe it was nothing more than the cool breeze of the air conditioned building that helped revived me. Regardless of the cause, I was feeling much more alert and awake. Rejuvenated, I struck up a conversation with one of the local artists who was working on some pipestone at a carving station. I began inquiring about the stone and where she had learned the techniques necessary to form the sacred stone into pipe. Like many other carvers, the skill was passed down from her mother, who had retired from carving after having spent over 30 years at the monument. For the past 12 years the woman had continued the family tradition of pipe carving. When I broached the topic of the little people, the talkative woman suddenly went quiet. This was not unusual; my experience with Native Americans is that they closely watch their words when discussing any topic of the supernatural. This quietness is not caused by rudeness, but by the reverence they hold for topics of the supernatural. With a little gentle prodding—and a sincere interest expressed in the topic—the woman eventually began to open up a bit. She told me that as a little girl she was told cautionary tales of the little people, advised to always treat them with respect and warned to never do anything that might anger them. Mainly she said that tribal elders seldom spoke at length about the little people due to their unwillingness to upset them and the possibility of facing the dire consequences. On a more personal level, she told me that very few people had actually caught sight of the little people; mostly people would catch a fast blur of something small passing through their peripheral vision. While working on the sacred pipestone, her mother would often get the sense that someone or something was keeping a close eye on her actions. Much to my amazement, the woman began sharing stories detailing the prankster nature of the little people, stating that one of the most frequently reported actions of the little people was their fondness to play with people's hair. On numerous occasions, both the woman and her mother would feel someone playfully tapping away at their head or tug at their hair, and without fail the culprit would never be identified. The more times this odd game was repeated, the more convinced the women became that the little people were responsible for the pranks. In a final statement, the woman strongly advised me against trying to call out or entice the little people into make themselves known, because I would most certainly not like their reaction. Not wanting to give the woman alarm, I decided it best if I kept my unexplained session of drowsiness to myself.

Author Bio

Chad Lewis – Is a researcher, author, and lecturer on topics of the strange and unusual. He has a Master of Science Degree in Psychology and has trekked across the world in search of the paranormal. From tracking vampires in Transylvania and chasing the Chupacabras in Puerto Rico, to searching for the elusive monster in Loch Ness, and pursuing ghosts in Ireland's castles, Chad brings over 16 years of research experience to his work.

Chad has been featured on the Discovery Channel's "A Haunting," ABC's "World's Scariest Places," and hundreds of radio interviews, TV appearances, and newspaper articles. Chad is also the author and co-author of numerous books on the strange and unusual.

To reach Chad, go to his websites:

www.unexplainedresearch.com or www.chadlewisresearch.com

You can also email him at chadlewis44@hotmail.com

Other Titles Authored/Co-Authored by Chad Lewis

Haunted Places

The Illinois Road Guide to Haunted Locations

The Iowa Road Guide to Haunted Locations

The Florida Road Guide to Haunted Locations

The Minnesota Road Guide to Haunted Locations

The South Dakota Road Guide to Haunted Locations

The Wisconsin Road Guide to Haunted Locations

Haunted St. Paul

General Paranormal

Hidden Headlines of New York

Hidden Headlines of Texas

Hidden Headlines of Wisconsin

The Wisconsin Road Guide to Mysterious Creatures

Gangsters

The Minnesota Road Guide to Gangster Hot Spots

The Wisconsin Road Guide to Gangster Hot Spots